BIBLICAL DIRECTIONISM:

A BIBLICAL APPROACH TO COUNSELING METHODOLOGY

DENNIS D. FREY, TH.D.

GMA & INSPIRATION PRESS
NEWBURGH, INDIANA

ISBN:

GMA and Inspiration Press, Newburgh, Indiana, in cooperation with Master's Library Press.

GMAPublishing.com
Check out our website.
GMA is a global publishing company.
Our books are available and distributed around the world and can be found on the internet at Amazon, Barnes and Noble and any major bookseller.

GMAPublishing@aol.com

Manuscript Assistant and Cover by: Ruth E. Parker
Just Imaginations
www.justimaginations.com

Printed in the United States of America

FORWORD

Dr. Frey has provided the Nouthetic Counselor some new terms to express old concepts. He has suggested a structure, or pattern, by which the biblical counselor can practice the Nouthetic model. He has argued puissantly for the purity of the biblical model and raised afresh the thorny question of authority for the Christian who would counsel with eclectic or integrated models.

His work should be viewed as complimentary to the pioneering work of Dr. Jay Adams. Dr. Adams has been to Christian counseling what Luther was to soteriology and harmartiology. Dr. Frey, like the second generation Reformers, has provided a systemization of the work which has preceded him. Or, to use Dr. Adams' own imagery, Frey has contributed to that building for which Adams constructed the superstructure.

As a second-generation biblical counselor myself, I commend Dr. Frey for his contribution. It is my prayer that his work will facilitate the adoption and implementation of the biblical (nouthetic) counseling model by many Christian professional and lay counselors.

May God be glorified and His people benefited as this work contributes to the equipping of the saints.

Howard A. Eyrich, D.Min.
Birmingham, Alabama

Contents

APPLIED DEFINITION OF KEY TERMS iii

INTRODUCTION vi

CHAPTER I
DERIVATION OR SUPERIMPOSITION?
Christian Counseling vs. Biblical Counseling
Methodological Development 1-9

CHAPTER II
BIBLICAL DIRECTIONISM COUNSELING:
A DERIVATIVE SYSTEM OF COUNSELING 10-28

CHAPTER III
BIBLICAL DIRECTIONISM COUNSELING
STEP ONE: DETERMINATIVE PROFILING 29-38

CHAPTER IV
BIBLICAL DIRECTIONISM COUNSELING
STEP TWO: COMPARATIVE SILHOUETTING 39-52

CHAPTER V
BIBLICAL DIRECTIONISM COUNSELING
STEP THREE: REDEMPTIVE CONFRONTATION 53-62

CHAPTER VI
BIBLICAL DIRECTIONISM COUNSELING
STEP FOUR: INDIVIDUAL COMMITMENT 63-73

CHAPTER VII
BIBLICAL DIRECTIONISM COUNSELING
STEP FIVE: PERSONAL CONDITIONING 74-90

CONCLUSION 91

APPENDIX 92-112

ABOUT THE AUTHOR 113

BIBLIOGRAPHY 114-116

APPLIED DEFINITION OF KEY TERMS

COUNSELING REGIME (CONCEPT)

A counseling regime (concept), is a regular pattern or course of action taken by a counselor in the practice of counseling which is the result of his/her general idea concerning what constitutes an appropriate counseling process.

> **EXAMPLE:** When Jim Doe counsels he uses a non-confrontational approach based upon his belief in a non-directed approach to client-centered therapy. The potential for various counseling regimes (concepts) may be nearly limitless.

PHYSIOLOGICAL CONSTANTS

A physiological constant is a known uniform characteristic whereby predictable certain functions of mind and body interact in a generally accepted manner.

> **EXAMPLE:** Excessive mental anxiety may produce physical manifestations, e.g. peptic ulcers, headaches, high blood pressure. Blushing may be the result of extreme excitement or embarrassment. Fear may result in temporary physical paralysis.

RATIONE ET VIA CERTUS

This Latin phrase translates: "The method which is infallible." **RATIONE ET VIA**. "The method". **CERTUS**. "Certain or infallible."

> **APPLICATION:** As applied in this study **RATIONE ET VIA CERTUS** refers to the Scripture as the source for the counseling methodology which is infallible.

SUPERIMPOSITION

A superimposition refers to the process whereby two or more counseling models are integrated into a single counseling motif resulting in one model being in prominence.

> **EXAMPLE:** Jane Smith has studied several counseling models. She is fully convinced of man's evolutionary ascent, but only partially agrees with Freud's conclusions. While she has come to appreciate a non-directed approach to counseling, she still feels it is necessary to guide the counselee toward successful closure. As a result, while her counseling method involves not actually telling the client what to do, she does dominate the direction in which she allows the counselee to go. In addition, she encourages the counselee to accept personal responsibility for certain actions, but assures him that there are no real absolutes in making life choices.

DERIVATION

A derivation refers to the process whereby a counseling model is developed from a single or greatly restricted source. While a derivation may recognize certain physiological constants germane to most other counseling models, integration with differing models is rigorously avoided.

> **EXAMPLE:** Bill Jones is totally committed to the concepts of Carl Rogers, and uses only Rogers' principles in his counseling. He is thus known as a "Rogerian" counselor. Betty Doe believes that Carl

Rogers was mostly wrong in his approach to counseling. Her training has led her to adopt the teachings and practices of Abraham Maslow. As a disciple of Maslow she specializes in "self-actualizing" counseling. The same may be said of those who are strict disciples of Erik Erikson, B.F. Skinner, or Sigmund Freud.

NOTE: All Scripture references are quoted from the New International Version (NIV) of the Bible, Grand Rapids, The Zondervan Corporation. Where used, KJV is the abbreviation for the King James Version of the Bible.

INTRODUCTION

The genesis of this counseling model came in three distinct steps. The first was a matter of necessity. As a newly minted pastor, I quickly found my "pastoral counseling" training as inadequate as my personal skills. After many failings, the Spirit of God impressed upon my heart the need to seek out solutions from Scripture as an alternative to my feeble attempts at what may be termed "Christian psycho-reason."

The second step came when Scriptural reason demonstrated a remarkable power to actually bring about literal change in the lives of those coming for counsel. Not only so, but also to draw these individuals away from me as a counselor and toward the Lord Jesus Christ...the giver of life and freedom.

The final step was as much a matter of necessity as the first. Gradually, it became clear that not only had God provided us with the answers, He had also provided a method by which the answers could be brought to bear within the human heart. That is, within the Scriptures was a defined system of counseling. Actually, a step-by-step sequence that took the "guess work" out of "how" to counsel and accepted that the Creator had given both His Word and the way in which His Word is best planted in the mind and heart.

Therefore, it is the goal of this text to present (not invent) this system in such a way as to make it so clear that it becomes obvious that the author is only a student of the Word accepting biblical basics. This thought may be better expressed in the following anecdote:

After a "courtesy reading" of the original manuscript for this work, Dr. Richard Meier observed, "Dennis, there is nothing really new here. In fact, I have been counseling this way for many years. I just never thought to assign definitions to the steps. It is rather the natural way to do Biblical counseling." I agreed with Dr. Meier. I trust that you, the reader, will agree as well. *Solo de Gloria!*

CHAPTER I

DERIVATION OR SUPERIMPOSITION

ANY GIVEN COUNSELING MODEL is the product of some form of synthesis. This synthesis combines the elements of research in such a way as to develop an acceptable standard by which a counseling model may be developed. Thus, the resulting regime (concept or model) benefits from the derivation of observable data collected in the research and development process. More plainly, counseling models are conglomerates.

When multiple models are integrated, a type of superimposition takes place, in that the positive elements of one model are placed in prominence over the negative or weaker elements of another model. Thus, the synthesis may result in overlapping motifs.[1] The superimposition of one concept over that of another is, in part, due to the fact that there are certain concepts shared by all counseling models.[2] These shared concepts are often integrated into the synthesis.

What separates a derived counseling regime from that of a superimposed concept is the degree to which integration has taken place. For example, the integration of "talk therapy" with "behavior therapy"[3] results in a superimposed concept. Though one therapy regime may be influenced by another, the dominant concept will be in prominence. The resulting synthesis will be a therapy based upon one primary motif with elements of the secondary being integrated into the whole.

A derivation, while sharing many of those concepts held by all counseling models (e.g. sensation)[4], remains largely the product of a single major theme. An example would be the psychoanalytic technique built entirely upon a Freudian motif.[5]

1

The question of derivation or superimposition is not
usually a major issue (if an issue at all) among secular
counselors. Primarily, this is due to a general belief
among secular counselors that no system of absolutes
exists. Consequently, any given model may be as valid
as another.

While such an attitude may be acceptable among
certain academicians and therapists, it must be rejected
by anyone who believes in a system of absolutes. It is
at this very juncture that the dichotomy between biblical
counseling and secular counseling is most apparent.[6]

CHRISTIAN COUNSELING
VS.
BIBLICAL COUNSELING

There is a great deal of tension between the terms
"Christian Counseling" and "Biblical Counseling." This
difference may at first seem only semantic; It is, in
fact, diametric. One may very well profess to be a
Christian counselor, all the while holding to a
synthesis of counseling which is almost wholly
diametrically opposed to the basic tenets of the
Christian faith.[7] Biblical counseling, on the other
hand, accepts only those psychological concepts
which are germane to the physiological constants
built within all legitimate psychological models.[6]

CHRISTIANS WHO COUNSEL

The counseling establishment is so diverse it almost
defies any reasonable containment. However, primary
among counselors would be practicing clinical
psychiatrists and psychologists, clinical social workers,
and that nearly indefinable collection of counseling
professionals from a broad spectrum of the mental
health field. Within these diverse professions, are
Christians who are working at every level.

The degree to which the Christian who counsels holds to one counseling model or another, depends not so much upon background and training (though that certainly plays an important part) but more so as to how strongly that Christian views the authority of the Bible and its adequacy as a "Handbook" for the human mind. Otherwise, the individual's Christian faith becomes merely a general format over which any given number of psychological concepts may be superimposed.

This thought is poignantly illustrated by Christian psychologist William Kirk Kilpatrick. He says, "*In fact, when people hear that I'm involved with both psychology and Christianity, they generally assume I'm working on a synthesis to bring the two closer together, to patch up whatever remaining differences there might be. 'Aren't psychology and religion just two different ways of getting at the same thing?' It's a question I often hear.*"[9]

Dr. Kilpatrick goes on to make the point even more clearly when he observes, "*It is true that popular psychology shares much in common with Eastern religion; in fact, a merger is well under way. But if you're talking about Christianity, it is much truer to say that psychology and religion are competing faiths. If you seriously hold to one set of values, you logically have to reject the other.*"[10]

Kilpatrick's idea of "competing faiths" is well illustrated in **THE PSYCHOLOGY OF MENTAL HEALTH**, written many years ago by Louis P. Thorpe. Though somewhat dated in terms of publication, Thorpe, nevertheless, expresses quite well what is still the prevailing attitude within the secular psychological establishment. In chapter seventeen, which he devotes to the subject of "Religion, Ethics, and Mental Health," Thorpe comments rather tersely on the matter of biblical norms.

"*Religious groups which...over-emphasize the threat of 'sin' and the rewards of the supposed 'life hereafter' as a*

*substitute for enjoyment of life in the present are likely
to foster mental ill health.*

*Another aspect of the last named problem is that of
utilizing religion as a means escape from reality or as a
dependency mechanism which encourages the
individual to 'cast his burdens on the Lord' and cease to
do anything about them himself.*"[11]

Even a superficial examination of the above statement
reveals a most serious incongruence between Biblical
Christianity and secular psychology. Thus, the
Christian who counsels is faced with a serious dilemma.

THE PROBLEM OF INTEGRATION

In Webster's Ninth New Collegiate Dictionary, "integrate"
is defined as, "to form, coordinate, or blend into a
functioning or unified whole."[12] The question for the
Christian counselor is whether or not he or she is willing
to blend secular systems with biblical Christianity. When
we speak here of "secular systems" we are not referring
to those psychological norms which are recognized as
physiological constants (noted earlier.)[13]

The inevitable results of superimposing the secular upon
the sacred is to weaken the sacred and strengthen the
secular. Again, Kilpatrick's insights are collaborative.

*"For someone schooled in the psychological tradition,
the Christian counselor must appear as scandalous.
'My whole heart?' 'My whole strength?' Psychology is not
comfortable with this kind of talk and wants frightfully
to water the whole thing down to a more palatable
formula. Some Christians will follow the psychological
lead and do the same."*[14]

THERAPY OR ADVICE?

Where the question of integration is taken seriously, an unusual division often results. The Christian counselor who integrates may consider his counseling regime to be "therapy," that is, "treatment of the emotionally disturbed." This may include secular systems such as nondirective therapy, psychoanalysis, hypnotherapy, psychodrama, or some form of group therapy.[15]

The Christian counselor who rejects integration and holds seriously to a derivative form of biblical counseling, may be seen as something less than a therapist and something more as a giver of advice. That is, someone who must not be taken too seriously as a *bona fide* therapist. For example, the secular counselor who suggests his client should not be overly distraught because of his deviate sexual desires, may be seen as a therapist offering affirmation and healing. Whereas, the biblical counselor who advises his client to seek the forgiveness of God, and begin to systematically restructure his thinking according to biblical principles, may be viewed as giving only advice and perhaps inappropriate advice at that!

METHODOLOGICAL DEVELOPMENT

The various counseling methods (models), most widely accepted within the field of psychology, are actually the synthesis of a methodological development of one sort or another. The degree to which clinical and theoretical development were involved varies, although clinical development certainly dominates.[16]

The methodological development of secular systems is based upon the Darwinian presupposition that man is the biological apex of evolutionary forces. Freud, though not as blindly accepted today as in the past, is nevertheless the primary foundational figure in secular methodological development.

The impact of Darwin's evolutionary thesis upon Freud's thinking was profound, even elemental, to his understanding of the human mind.[17] The resulting Darwinian/Freudian influence upon present day counseling methods presents a dilemma for the Christian counselor.

THE PROBLEM OF CHOICES

One of the choices open to Christians who counsel is the adoptive synthesis of integration. In the *milieu* of potential models, integration can appear to be a legitimate alternative to what may be otherwise viewed as "professional suicide" if one fails to adopt prevailing norms.

But how does the Christian make such a choice? If the secular models are built entirely upon an evolutionary premise, then any regime, model, method, or concept borrowed from secular methodological development is likely to be suspect from the beginning. Thinking about it very much leaves one with the sense that there is an irresolvable conflict between biblical principles and so much of secular psychology.[18]

PROFESSIONAL PRESSURE

That a conflict exists is hardly debatable. The problem, however, is not whether there is a conflict, but in how that conflict can be resolved. One method of resolution is integration; another is rejection of all but those physiological constants spoken of earlier and a quest for the derivation of a biblical methodology that is not superimposed upon by secular systems. Such a quest is difficult, and the application of any derived methodology even more difficult. There are many reasons for such difficulties, not the least of which is professional peer pressure.

The obtaining of state licensure and acceptance into professional fraternities usually hinges upon one's acquaintance with, and knowledge of, the major secular systems. Failure to integrate such systems into one's own counseling motif could very well result in a damaging estrangement from one's own professional peers.[19]

ACCEPTING BIBLICAL BASICS

One place for the Christian mental health professional to begin is to adopt an unwavering confidence in biblical basics. That is, that the Bible is the authoritative and infallible Word of God to man. As such, it may be understood as the "how to" manual for the human mind.

Usually, there is little conflict between the secularist and the Christian when the secularist is suggesting that some principle of the Bible is congruent with prevailing theory. As long as the Scriptures are not given credit for being preemptive, the secularist is usually content to adopt a benign if not supportive attitude toward the biblical position.

What the biblical counselor suggests is quite different. The biblical counselor insists that the Scriptural standard is authoritative and final. Consequently, any congruence on the part of the secular system is either a type of natural plagiarism or a re-invention of already established truth.

Developing total confidence in the Bible does not negate the need to study secular systems. Neither does such confidence alone render one totally competent to counsel. What it does, however, is to establish that singular source of truth from which an infallible counseling methodology may be derived.

Chapter I

Questions for Review

1 In your own words, discriminate between a counseling model which is derived and one that is superimposed.

_____

_____

_____

_____

_____

2 Explain how Christian counseling may differ from biblical counseling.

_____

_____

_____

_____

_____

3 What does the term "integration" generally imply as it relates to Christians who counsel?

_____

_____

_____

_____

_____

4 Explain your present philosophy regarding "integration" as defined in Chapter One.

_____

_____

_____

_____

_____

ENDNOTES

CHAPTER I

1 Hall, Calvin S. and Nordby, Vernon J., 1972, <u>A Guide to Psychologists and Their Concepts</u>. (San Francisco, California: W.H. Freeman and Company), 3-4.
2 *Ibid.*, 4.
3 Hill, Winfred, 1970, <u>Psychology: Principles and Problems</u>. (New York: J.B.Lippincott Company, 632-635.
4 *Ibid*, 161-162.
5 Menninger, Karl, 1961, <u>Theory of Psychoanalytic Technique</u>. (New York: Science Editions, Inc.), 3-4.
6 Adams, Jay E., 1970, <u>Competent to Counsel</u>, (Phillipsburg, New Jersey: Presbyterian and Reformed Publishing House), xi-xii of Introduction.
7 *Ibid*, xi-xii of Introduction.
8 Hill, *Op. cit.*, 29-53.
9 Kilpatrick, William Kirk, 1983, <u>Psychological Seduction</u>. (New York: Thomas Nelson Publishers), 13-14.
10 *Ibid*, 14.
11 Thorpe, Louis P., 1960, <u>The Psychology of Mental Health</u>. (New York: The Ronald Press Company), 506.
12 Hill, *Op. cit.*, 29-53.
13 Kilpatrick, *Op. cit.*, 15.
14. *Ibid*, 232.
15 Thorpe, *Op. cit.*, 242-249.
16 Hall & Nordby, *Op. cit.*, 3-4.
17 Jones, Ernest, 22-30.
18 Kilpatrick, *Op. cit.*, 14.
19 Hill, *Op. cit.*, 628-632.

CHAPTER II

BIBLICAL DIRECTIONISM COUNSELING
A DERIVATIVE SYSTEM OF COUNSELING

IN CHAPTER ONE, it was suggested that a derivative counseling methodology, while incorporating those physiological constants accepted within most (if not all) counseling models, was rather free standing in that it was built upon one primary premise from which the entire derivative system was synthesized.

BIBLICAL DIRECTIONISM is the name chosen to represent the synthesis of a methodological development which claims as its foundational premise, a single non-negotiable element primary to all the research and development conducted toward the synthesis.

THE FOUNDATIONAL PREMISE

The foundational premise, upon which Biblical Directionism counseling is built, is that the sixty-six canonized books of the Old and New Testament Bible constitute the infallible Word of God to man. As such, they represent and contain all truth necessary for the proper development, correction, and maintenance of the human mind. This foundational premise is firmly established in the Bible itself. The following passages, while certainly not exhaustive, are representative.

> *"The Law of the Lord is perfect, reviving the soul. The statutes of the Lord are trustworthy, making wise the simple. The precepts of the Lord are right, giving joy to the heart. The commands of the Lord are radiant, giving light to the eyes."*
> Psalm 19:7-8.

*"How can a young man keep his way
pure? By living according to Your Word."*
Psalm 119:9

*"The grass withers and the flowers fall, but
the Word of our God stands forever."*
Isaiah 40:8

*"All Scripture is God breathed and is
useful for teaching, rebuking, correcting,
and training in righteousness, so that the
man of God may be thoroughly equipped
for every good work."* II Timothy 3:16-17

*"For the Word of God is living and active.
Sharper than any doubled-edged sword,
it penetrates even to dividing soul and
spirit, joints and morrow; it judges the
thoughts and attitudes of the heart."*
Hebrews 4:12

That the Scriptures represent themselves to be an adequate handbook for the human mind can hardly be argued. Existing support for Scriptural integrity is another issue.

SCRIPTURAL INTEGRITY

Of its own integrity, the Scripture testifies: "The statutes of the Lord are trustworthy" Psalm 19:7. "The grass withers and the flowers fall, but the Word of our God stands forever." Isaiah 40:8. Nevertheless, critical thinking compels one to seek additional proofs which independently collaborate without collusion.

11

The proof, then, hinges upon the question of "infallibility," or whether the Bible actually is totally without error. The question has been succinctly articulated in the following statement.

"To many thoughtful conservatives, the greatest weakness...lies in the lack of an adequate view of the inspiration of the Bible. Are the Scriptures to be thought of as merely the human witness to divine revelation, subject to error as other human productions, their record to be judged merely as other ancient writings are to be judged? Is the Bible the Word of God in itself or only when and to the degree that God uses it to confront us by His Spirit in the reading and preaching of the Scriptures. Can we really have a revelation without a Bible which is doctrinally inerrant and factually trustworthy?"[1]

In answer to this question, Rousas J. Rushdoony has suggested:

"The biblical philosophy is grounded on the doctrine of the infallibility of Scripture. A God who is struggling together with man against the darkness of a universe of brute factuality is a God who is struggling to realize himself. He cannot, therefore, speak predicatively but only hopefully, because he is not in total control. Again, because he has not fully realized himself, he is not fully self-conscious, so that his word lacks perspicuity and lucidity; it cannot be infallible, because he is neither perfect, omnipotent, nor sovereign. It can merely be an inspiring exhortation from another leading 'freedom fighter.'"[2]

When one considers the sobriety of Rushdoony's observation, it becomes clear that the concept of Scriptural infallibility may be predicated upon something in addition to the witness of the Bible (that is not to suggest that the Bible is in any manner an inadequate witness of its own infallibility). While not intending to give support to all of Rushdoony's views on biblical authority, he has, nevertheless, contributed significantly to a helpful criticism of the conservative view of Scriptural inspiration. His insight at this point is helpful.

> *"But the orthodox doctrine holds to the infallible Word because it recognizes that God created all things, governs all things, and knows all things, and 'known unto God are all His works, from the beginning of the world.' (Acts 15:18). A perfect, omnipotent, and totally self-conscious God can only speak infallibly; His Word is inescapably an infallible Word."*[3]

The integrity of the Bible does not rest exclusively upon human participation in either the original autographs or the work of preservation. Ultimately, the integrity of the Bible must rest upon the integrity of God Himself. Either God is, or He is not. If He is, then He is God, and His capacity to present and preserve His Word to mankind cannot be increased or decreased. Beyond this barrier to belief, one cannot go except by faith. No one has ever said it better than the writer of the Book of Hebrews (though admittedly a biblical witness). "And without faith it is impossible to please God, because anyone who comes to Him must believe that He exists and that He rewards those who earnestly seek Him." Hebrews 11:6.

While the whole matter of Scriptural infallibility rests ultimately upon the prerogative of faith, it does not rest there devoid of either internal or external support. The integrity of the biblical record has been systematically vindicated down through the centuries. No other written document in the history of mankind has been the subject of such intense scrutiny as has the Bible.

It is also quite reasonable to suggest that the more one knows of true science, the more respect one has for the integrity of the Bible. This fact is especially confirming as it relates to the relatively new science of archaeology that has provided an almost inexhaustible supply of validating and vindicating proofs of biblical integrity, without invalidating a single fact of biblical historicity.[4]

What is said here of archaeology may be said also of linguistics, hermeneutics, biology, anthropology, psychology, cosmology, astronomy, thermodynamics, physics, geology, and a host of other scientific disciplines.[5]

BIBLICAL AUTHORITY

Biblical Directionism counseling prefaces its entire methodology upon the belief that the Bible is authoritative in all its dealings with man. Warren C. Young has stated this philosophy quite well.

> *"Christian philosophy begins, then with the assertion of a positive, supernatural, and authoritative message. This message is never to be thought of as a human achievement but always as a divine gift. It is a Word which comes to man from an order beyond the world of natural experience. It is a Word directed toward the whole man, to his emotions, his intellect, and his will, not to any one aspect of his personality."[6]*

The place of Scripture in the development of a methodological derivative, such as Biblical Directionism counseling, is total. The authority of the Bible is seen as over the whole of the affairs of man. Therefore, it will permeate every area of counseling technique and therapy in a redemptive, supportive, and directive fashion.

Even Christian psychotherapists, who are not specifically schooled in the use of Scripture as an authoritative absolute, find it difficult to avoid using the Bible in this very manner.

Dr. O. Quentin Hyder observed:

> *"There really is something different about Christian psychotherapy if that difference is the additional power and influence of God mediated by the Holy Spirit. As I have increased in confidence and experience, I have felt more and more free to integrate Scriptural principles into the strategy and tactics of psychotherapy that I learned while in training. Quoting or reading from the Bible is frequently not only appropriate, but often freshly illuminating and helpful to patients."*[7]

While integrating Scriptures into some other system of psychotherapy may seem harmless (even preferable), it is precisely the dilemma that the biblical counselor must seek to avoid. We are referring here, again, to the problems associated with superimposition.

BIBLICAL SUFFICIENCY

It is the contention of Biblical Directionism counseling that the Bible is, in and of itself, a sufficiently adequate source book on the human mind; and, as such, constitutes a sufficient reservoir out of which a methodological derivative may be synthesized. This is what is meant by *biblical sufficiency.*

Not only is the Scripture viewed as sufficient, more importantly, it is viewed as obligatory. Jay E. Adams has correctly pointed this out.

> *"The Holy Spirit expects counselors to use His Word, the Holy Scriptures...He gave it for such a purpose...it is powerful when used for that purpose. His counseling work is ordinarily performed through the ministry of this Word."*[8]

This sufficiency is clearly indicated in II Timothy 3:16-17.

> *"All Scripture is God-breathed and is useful for teaching, rebuking, correcting, and training in righteousness, so that the man of God may be thoroughly equipped for every good work."*

It is the chief calling of man to live righteously under God.[9] Unless that calling is fulfilled, there can be no mental health. In fact, it is this very calling that seeks to establish the mind as healthy. For the establishment of a healthy mind, the Scriptures are sufficient.

THE DERIVATIVE SYSTEM

The methodological development of Biblical Directionism counseling is the result of a derivative synthesis of the biblical principles of counseling. Three fundamental questions served as the motivator for the system. These were:

1. Is the Bible an adequate source book on the human mind? That is, does it contain sufficient information for the development of a counseling methodology; and is that information in the form of a complete and unified whole?

2. Can the complete and unified whole be synthesized into a recognizable counseling methodology?

3. Does the methodological development result in a derivative synthesis that is both coherent and logical?

Unless the Bible constitutes an adequate source book on the human mind (and consequently, human behavior), is amendable to reasonable development, and results in a logical approach, it cannot possibly be accepted as a valid constitution for the formulation of a viable counseling model. If, on the other hand, it can meet these requirements, it is clearly the **RATIONE ET VIA CERTUS**.

THE ADEQUACY OF SCRIPTURE

Christian psychologist, Dr. William Bacus, has stated:

> *"The Scriptures teach that we don't have to be content with relative truth. We can actually know ultimate truth about reality. In fact, we can even have a personal relationship with God Himself through the life, death, and resurrection of Jesus Christ. When we believe this, the Spirit of Truth literally teaches us truth through the Word of God. When a person comes to believe the truth and actually cognizes it (uses it to live by), that person will experience emotional and behavioral consequences which are truly positive and healthful."*[10]

In this statement, Dr. Bacus is recognizing the revelation of the truth in our Lord Jesus' statements: "If you hold to My teachings, then you are really My disciples. Then you will know the truth, and the truth will set you free." John 8:31-32. "Your (God's) Word is Truth." John 17:17. The teachings of the Lord Jesus and all that is quantifiable of God cannot be known, nor have they been revealed outside of Scripture. Hence, the

Scriptures are the only adequate and structured repository of absolute (ultimate), truth.

The word "absolute" is considered objectionable to a great many individuals within the academic and scientific disciplines. WEBSTER'S NINTH NEW COLLEGIATE DICTIONARY lists ten related definitions for the word "absolute". The primary definition is: "free from imperfections." It is this definition that is herein applied. Restated, it may be said that the Bible is the only repository of truth that is free from imperfection. Stated in this manner, it may seem redundant to suggest that truth may be absolute. Seemingly, either it is truth or it is not. However, when one considers that truth may also be viewed relatively, the term "absolute truth" is both reasonable and instructive.

The testimony of the Bible itself is that it represents absolute truth; and if absolute, then certainly adequate. The word "adequate" is defined here as, "sufficient for a specific requirement." Thus, the Scriptures being the only repository of absolute truth, constitute the only source-book of information which is fully sufficient for meeting the specific requirement of a totally trustworthy derivative counseling methodology.

Again, we consider a statement from Dr. William Bacus:

> *"Let us suppose you are going to try to change the thoughts in some 'black box' by rooting out a person's misbeliefs (sic) and replacing them with the truth. What can you use as a guide or criterion to determine what is true and what isn't? The Christian criterion for the contents of the black box is the truth of God. That is, of course the criterion Jesus Himself recommended. And in the Christian view of things, the ultimate source of the distortions and irrationalities*

18

*which disorder human lives is the devil.
Thus, the Scriptures offer their own
criteria for behavior and their own use
of "cognitive therapy."*[11]

Dr. Bacus' statement is congruent with the premise of
Biblical Directionism counseling, which is: The system
accepts, without equivocation, the belief that the
sixty-six books of the Old and New Testament
Scriptures constitute the only certain and accurate
source of information regarding the answers to life's
most perplexing problems. It further accepts the belief
that if these answers are honestly and faithfully applied
to the individual life, they will assure the highest and
most meaningful existence possible.

EXPOSITIONAL DEVELOPMENT

Having established the adequacy of Scripture, the next
step is to seek a method by which the complete and
unified whole of the Bible can be synthesized into a
recognizable and comprehensible methodology. In
other words, how can this repository of absolute truth
be methodically formulated into a systematic and
comprehensive counseling procedure.

"Exposition" is defined here as: "a discourse or an
example of it designed to convey information or
explain what is difficult to understand." By
"expositional development," it is meant that the
Scriptural whole is reduced to a synthesis which
renders the complex body of truth contained therein
into a certain form which is compatible with a logical
and workable counseling methodology.

THE SYSTEM LOGIC

Logic, as applied in this context, is defined as: "the
interrelation or sequence of facts or events when seen

as inevitable or predictable." It is the logic of Biblical Directionism counseling that the Bible, as the repository of absolute truth and as an adequate source book for dealing with the human mind, ought to inevitably contain a methodological system that is predictable and verifiable.

Thus, it seems reasonable that a logical methodology does, in fact, exist as a coherent system within the whole of the Scriptures. The remaining step being that of developing a derivative system by reason of a viable synthesis.

THE DERIVATIVE SYNTHESIS

The question of how to derive a counseling methodology from an almost overwhelming bulk of biblical data is not an easy one to answer. The fact that theological diversity exists on every major biblical doctrine is demonstrative of the difficulties involved in any biblical interpretation; and, after all, synthesis inescapably involves interpretation.

Therefore, in attempting to arrive at a derivative synthesis, a hermeneutical approach was employed. However, a hermeneutical approach to synthesis need not degenerate into an exercise in merely subjective interpretation.

Properly speaking, hermeneutics is: "the study of those principles which pertain to the interpretation of Holy Scriptures...hermeneutics is both an art and a science. It is a science in that it can reduce interpretation within limits to a set of rules; it is an art in that, not infrequently, elements in the text escape easy treatment by rules. Some writers have argued that the giving and taking of meaning in understanding (Verstehen) is more art than science. But at least it is not all art, and what is not art can be treated by rule."12

In keeping with Ramm's definition of hermeneutics, both science and art were employed in the methodological development of the derivative synthesis we have identified as **BIBLICAL DIRECTIONISM COUNSELING**; and, as will be demonstrated, the careful use of interpretation has guarded its development.

DEVELOPING A WORKING MODEL

The term "Biblical Directionism" was chosen to represent a counseling system based upon the principles and truths revealed in the Bible. The word "direction" is herein defined as:

(a.) "a guidance or supervision of conduct";

(b.) "assistance in pointing out the proper route."

Thus, Biblical Directionism Counseling seeks to point the individual to God's Word for accurate and dependable guidance, supervision, and assistance.

However, for a system to be more than theory, it must be developed into a working model. Developing a working model, in the context of this approach, does not refer to some superimposed methodology upon the collective body of biblical truth...that would only result in one more flawed superimposition which violates the Scriptures by utilizing them as a convenient theme. Arriving at a working model, in the context of this approach, refers to the methodological development of a working model that is the actual derivative synthesis of the three questions postulated earlier in this chapter. They are:

1. Is the Bible an adequate source book on the human mind? That is, does it contain sufficient information for the development of a counseling methodology, and is that information in the form of a complete and verifiable whole?

2. Can the complete and verifiable whole be synthesized into a recognizable counseling methodology?

3. Does the methodological development result in a derivative synthesis that is both coherent and logical?

SETTING UP AN APPROACH

For the development of a proper working model, the following question was postulated: "Is there a generic biblical method of counseling; and if there is, how does it work?" From this postulate, an approach is suggested. This approach is simple; it is designed to answer the postulate in the clearest and most uncomplicated manner. The resulting methodological development culminates in a derivative synthesis which takes on the form of a working model consisting of five distinct, yet inter-related, steps to counseling. These five steps involve the entire counseling process, from initiation to closure. Five foundational requisites form a platform from which the actual five steps are actuated.

FIVE FOUNDATIONAL REQUISITES

The system's five steps must be prefaced by several foundational requisites. These foundational requisites are:

I THE SYSTEM'S GUIDING PRINCIPLE

"All Scripture is God-breathed and is useful for teaching, rebuking, correcting and training in righteousness, so that the man of God may be thoroughly equipped for every good work." II Timothy 3:16-17.

II THE SYSTEM'S SCRIPTURAL MOTTO

"See to it that no one takes you captive through hollow and deceptive philosophy, which depends on human tradition and

*the basic principles of this world rather
than on Christ." Colossians 2:8.*

III   THE SYSTEM'S GOAL

Biblical Directionism counseling has as its
primary goal, the task of assisting the
counselee in becoming mentally and
spiritually whole.   This may be fully
accomplished only when the individual
enters into a right relationship with God.
Both mental and spiritual wholeness are
totally dependent upon one's personal
willingness to accept and act upon known
truth as revealed to them by God.   It is a
fundamental belief of the Christian faith
that this truth is inescapably revealed in the
Bible.   The goal of the biblical counselor
must be to present this truth to the
counselee in a manner which will facilitate
cognition and actualization.   Put bluntly,
without the born-again experience, the end
results of biblical counseling may
accomplish little more than to convince
the sinner to attempt to live a moral life.

IV THE SYSTEM'S STATEMENT OF BELIEF

It is an unchangeable law of God that
those who reject what they know to be
the truth of God will come ultimately to
ruin.   Genuine fulfillment in this life can
only be achieved in total submission to
the Creator as one willingly subordinates
his or her life to God's control.

V   THE SYSTEM'S STEPS AND SEQUENCE OF IMPLEMENTATION

The following five steps and sequence of
implementation are not the result of
forming Scripture around a previously
developed methodology. They are to be

understood as the result of recognizing the generic format of a biblically derived system of counseling procedures.

THE SYSTEM'S FIVE STEPS

STEP I   DETERMINATIVE PROFILING

Scriptural Premise: *"Let us examine our ways and test them..."* Lamentations 3:40.

DETERMINATIVE PROFILING is, broadly speaking, essentially data gathering. More specifically, Determinative Profiling is a biblically focused "examination" or "testing" of the individual's past and present state of being.

STEP II   COMPARATIVE SILHOUETTING

Scriptural Premise: *"For the Word of God is living and active. Sharper than any double-edged sword, it penetrates even to dividing soul and spirit, joints and marrow; it judges the thoughts and attitudes of the heart."* Hebrews 4:12.

COMPARATIVE SILHOUETTING is the process of using the data gathered during Determinative Profiling in such a way as to obtain an outline of the individual's past and present state of being over against that of the biblical norm. From this "comparative silhouette," a revealing picture is developed which, when assessed, will provide the counselor a base from which to determine counseling need and potential. This is because when the "Determinative Profile" which is essentially data, is contrasted with the "Comparative Silhouette," the result is the formation of biblically processed data into useful counseling information

STEP III   REDEMTIVE CONFRONTATION

Scriptural Premise: *"Will you judge them? Then confront them...and say to them: This is what the Sovereign Lord says:"* Ezekiel 20:4,5.

REDEMPTIVE CONFRONTATION involves both explanation and possible demonstration of how the individual's present state of being may be the result of the failure or success of having lived in accordance with the standards of God's Word.

Redemptive Confrontation may also involve pointing out what may be expected in the future as a consequence of obedience, or disobedience, to the standards of God's Word.

STEP IV   INDIVIDUAL COMMITMENT

Scriptural Premise: "Come unto Me, all you who are weary and burdened, and I will give you rest. Take my yoke upon you and learn of Me, for I am gentle and humble in heart, and you will find rest for your souls. For my yoke is easy and My burden is light." Matthew 11:28-30.

INDIVIDUAL COMMITMENT involves bringing the counselee face to face with the need to make a commitment to follow the biblical direction necessary for healing, spiritual rest, and individual wholeness.

STEP V   PERSONAL CONDITIONING

Scriptural Premise: "*They are to teach My people the difference between the holy and the common and show them how to distinguish between the unclean and the clean.*" Ezekiel 44:23.

PERSONAL CONDITIONING involves assisting the counselee in the initial process of putting into actual practice the biblical principles necessary for healing, spiritual rest, and personal wholeness, and confirming verification of this initial process.

The length of time necessary to fully implement each of these five steps depends upon a great many variables. Actual implementation may not always be chronologically proportional. Just as God deals with individuals in a fashion suited to their uniqueness, so will the five steps of Biblical Directionism counseling be implemented according to the uniqueness of the individual and his or her situation.

CHAPTER TWO

QUESTIONS FOR REVIEW

1 According to the author, upon what foundational principle does the entire concept of biblical integrity rest?

_____
_____
_____
_____
_____

2 What is meant by the term "Biblical Sufficiency"?

_____
_____
_____
_____
_____

3 Define the term, "Biblical Directionism".

_____
_____
_____
_____
_____

4 List the five basic steps of Biblical Directionism, and give a brief definition of each step.

_____
_____
_____
_____
_____

ENDNOTES

CHAPTER II

¹ Purkiser, W.T., 1955, <u>Exploring the Old Testament</u>. (Kansas City, MO: Beacon Hill Press of Kansas City), 68.

² Rushdoony, Rousas, 1979, <u>The Biblical Philosophy of History</u>. (Phillipsburg, N.J.: Presbyterian and Reformed Publishing Company), 8-9.

³ *Ibid*, 9.

⁴ Ramm, Bernard L. and Others, 1976, <u>Hermeneutics</u>. (Grand Rapids, MI: Braker Book House), 54-66.

⁵ For an exhaustive and contemporary treatment of the whole question of biblical integrity and modern science, see: Morris, Henry M., 1985, <u>The Biblical Basis For Modern Science</u>. (Grand Rapids, MI: Baker Book House).

⁶ Young, Warren C., 1982, <u>A Christian Approach to Philosophy</u>. (Grand Rapids, MI:Baker Book House), 201.

⁷ Hyder, O. Quentin, 1976, <u>The Christian's Handbook of Psychiatry</u>. (New York: Fleming H. Revell Company), 187.

⁸ Adams, Jay E., 1970, <u>Competent to Counsel</u>, (Phillipsburg, New Jersey: Presbyterian and Reformed Publishing House), 23.

⁹ Henry, Matthew, 1976, <u>Commentary on the Whole Bible</u>. (Ed. Leslie F. Church, Grand Rapids, MI: Zondervan Publishing House), 875-876.

¹⁰ Bacus, William, 1985, <u>Telling the Truth to Troubled People</u>. (Minneapolis, MN: Bethany House Publishers), 20.

¹¹ *Ibid*, 22.

¹² Ramm, *Op, cit.*, 8-9.

CHAPTER III

BIBLICAL DIRECTIONISM COUNSELING
STEP ONE:
DETERMINATIVE PROFILING

IN THE CONTEXT OF THIS PROCEDURE, a "profile" is defined as:
1) "a set of data often in graphic form portraying the significant features of something esp.: a graphic representing the extent to which an individual exhibits traits or abilities; 2) a concise biographical sketch." (WEBSTER'S NINTH NEW COLLEGIATE DICTIONARY.)

Determinative profiling is that initial step necessary for the formulation of a proper and viable determination of who the counselee is, what he/she has become, and where the "counselee" is at the present time in relation to his/her development as a human being.

The process of determinative profiling is initially an exercise in data gathering. Early on, it must be clear to the counselor that determinative profiling is for the purpose of gathering "data" and not "information." It is critical that the difference between "data" and "information" be clearly understood.

Data do not become information until they have passed through some system or unit of processing. The numbers "34602" may represent data only. Yes, it is true we may mistake these numbers for information. In fact, it can be argued that their very numerical values constitute information. However, this may not be useful information, only data. Realistically though, if we process the numbers "34602" into the sequence "63042" they can become informative, since they now represent the postal zip code of the a city in the United States. Determinative profiling is an exercise in data gathering. While these data may represent information, the biblical counselor must avoid processing data during this step. Data processing will be accomplished in the second step of Biblical Directionism counseling. To process data during the profiling stage is to almost certainly pass premature judgment. Premature judgment is actually "immature judgment" and in more cases than not, inaccurate judgment. In fact, the counselor has no authority to "pass judgment", as we shall later see.

This data gathering is an essential prerequisite to developing an accurate awareness of the counselee's true state of being. The need for such an accurate and unbiased awareness is two-fold. First, it is essential that the counselor really "know" the counselee's situation. Second, it is essential that the counselee really "know" his or her situation. As amazing as it may seem, many people in distress have lost sight of the relevant facts, and are suffering from what we might call "problem myopia."

As a proper consequence of determinative profiling, the counselee becomes better acquainted with his or her own state of being and is thus better able to understand the realities that surround him or her. As for the counselor, determinative profiling is essential to the prevention of premature judgment, misdiagnosis, and consequently, malpractice.

The methods employed in determinative profiling are essentially those common to any system of data gathering involving people. These may include questionnaires, tests, verbalizing, discussion, observation of body language, record retrieval, consultation with other professionals with whom the counselee may have had dealings, and whatever other legitimate methods may be properly employed. For the biblical counselor, one critical source of data is that which is provided by the insights afforded by the Holy Spirit.

Extreme caution must be exercised here, and the counselor must reject all notions of spiritual arrogance or pride, and humbly recognize that if the Holy Spirit chooses to assist him or her in the counseling process, it is only because it pleases the Holy Spirit to do so, and not because of some supposed merit earned by the counselor.

The process of comparative profiling is, in essence, a process of examination. By this it is meant that "examination" is a process whereby one is tested, inquired of, and carefully investigated in order to obtain a proper understanding of the relevant data of a given situation. By this action, the counselor is able to determine a profile of the counselee.

The acceptance of examination for the purpose of determinative profiling, as a first step in Biblical Directionism counseling, is based upon the belief that this is the entry point in all of God's dealings with man.

SCRIPTURAL METHODOLOGY

Essential to any meaningful cognition is the capacity and opportunity to know. Knowing is possible only when information is both available and recognized. Examination is that process whereby available information is made known and recognized. The result of such an examination is a revealing profile of who, what, and where the person's being really is.

The Scriptural premise from which this initial step is derived is found in the Book of Lamentations. "Let us examine our ways and test them..." Lamentations 3:40.

The Hebrew word translated "examine" in the NIV is translated "search" in the KJV. The word represented here is *hapas*, meaning, in this context, "to probe one's behavior."

The Hebrew word translated "test" in the NIV is translated "try" in the KJV. The word represented here is, *haqar*, meaning, in this context, "probing the heart, examining the mind." It can refer to initial phases of a search or the end result but always connotes a diligent, difficult probing.

WHY GOD SEEKS TO REACH MAN'S MIND

When the concept of profiling is delineated as it relates to this initial step of Biblical Directionism counseling, it must be understood the process of profiling is actually a tripartite event.[1] God desires to assist the biblical counselor in coming to know the counselee, while at the same time, assisting the counselee in coming to know himself or herself better through this process of data gathering.[2] The counselor desires to assist the counselee in coming to know himself or herself, yet is reliant upon God for real success.[3] The counselee hopes to know himself or herself better as he or she is directed and assisted by the counselor in the process of profiling, yet hopefully realizes that God is the ultimate source of wisdom in coming to terms with one's self.

Through this sometimes difficult, and always diligent, process of examination and testing an accurate and adequate individual profile is obtained. Without this profile, genuine knowing is impossible. Thus, it is essential to God's initial step of counseling the one comes to know who, what, and where he or she really is.

HOW GOD REACHES MAN'S MIND

Through this initial step of profiling, God reaches man's mind by employing the benefits of examination and testing in connection with man's God-created capacity to comprehend the known. Without the known results of examination and testing and a God-created capacity to comprehend the known, man could never move forward from any given state of being. Profiling, then, is that initial step of God's dealing with man whereby He makes it possible to change. That God uses human counselors in connection with this process is at once a given, and yet a mystery of His love.

Nevertheless, the practice of profiling is not limited to human counselors. No doubt millions have been taken through this initial step without the aid of human intervention. The directive intervention of the Holy Spirit is not dependent upon a third party human assistant.

However, it has pleased God to make use of human assistants in connection with His healing systems. How God accomplishes this is clearly revealed in Scripture.

EXPERIENTIAL METHODOLOGY

If profiling is to be called a generic initial step in proper biblical counseling, the Scriptures ought to abound with clear evidence of it. The following selections are only representative of a vast quantity of such evidence, but they do provide clear and concrete examples.

BIBLICAL CASE STUDIES

GOD COUNSELS ADAM AND THE WOMAN

> *"Then the man and his wife heard the sound of the Lord God as He was walking in the garden in the cool of the day, and they hid from the Lord God among the trees of the garden. But the Lord God called to the man, 'Where are you?' He answered, 'I heard You in the garden, and I was afraid because I was naked; so I hid.' And He said,, 'Who told you that you were naked? Have you eaten from the tree that I commanded you*

> **not to eat from?'** *The man said, 'The woman You put here with me --- she gave me some fruit from the tree, and I ate it.' Then the Lord said to the woman,* **'What is this you have done?'"** *Genesis 3:8-13.*

Data gathering began when God asked the first of several questions. In this case, profiling transcends mere data gathering and is actually instructive since it is obvious that the questions were not asked for God's benefit. Even in the case of human counselors, profiling can, and often is, an instructive tool as well as a data gathering process.

JOSEPH COUNSELS PHARAOH'S CUPBEARER AND BAKER

> *"When Joseph came to them the next morning, he saw that they were dejected. So he asked Pharaoh's officials who were in custody with him in his master's house;* **'Why are your faces so sad today?'** *'We both had dreams,' they answered, 'but there is no one to interpret them.' Then Joseph said to them, 'Do not interpretations belong to God?* **Tell me your dreams.'** *So the chief cupbearer told Joseph his dreams." Genesis 40:6-9a.*

Joseph began his counseling process by asking the question, "Why are your faces so sad today?" vs6. Before attempting to actually give counsel, he asked for further details, "Tell me your dreams." vs8. Not until Joseph was in possession of all the facts did he proceed to give counsel.

DANIEL COUNSELS NEBUCHADNEZZAR

"Finally, Daniel came into my presence and **I told him the dream**...I said...I know that the spirit of the holy gods is in you, and that no mystery is too difficult for you. **Here is my dream**; interpret it for me. **These are the visions I saw while lying on my bed:**" Daniel 4:8-10a.

Daniel is asked to interpret the king's dream. But notice the initial process of profiling: "I told him the dream." vs8. "Here is my dream." vs9; "These are the visions I saw." vs10a.

JESUS COUNSELS THE RICH YOUNG MAN

> *"Now a man came to Jesus and asked, 'Teacher, what good thing must I do to get eternal life?'* **'Why do you ask Me about what is good?** *There is only One Who is good. If you want to enter eternal life, obey the commandments.' 'Which ones?' the man inquired. Jesus replied, 'Do not murder; do not commit adultery; do not steal; do not give false testimony; honor your father and mother; love your neighbor as yourself.' 'All these I have kept,' the young man said. 'What do I still lack?'"* Matthew 19:16-20.

This young man came to Jesus for counsel. Notice Jesus' initial question, "Why do you ask Me about what is good?" vs17. Prior to giving actual counsel, Jesus leads the rich young man into further data gathering by exciting him to discuss his past. In so doing, the young man reveals a great deal about himself.

PREMIER CASE STUDY

NATHAN COUNSELS DAVID

> "The Lord sent Nathan to David. When he came to him, he said...." II Samuel 12:1a.

In this case, Nathan had already been through the process of profiling before ever approaching David. Notice: "The Lord sent Nathan to David." vs1a. God would not have permitted Nathan to approach David without knowing all of the facts of the case. A further reading of the narrative reveals that Nathan was in possession of the entire background and facts surrounding this most important case.

While present-day counselors would be foolish to presume that God would give the kind of "inside information" He granted to Nathan, it is nonetheless true that the genuine biblical counselor may expect that God's Holy Spirit will be directly involved in the data gathering process, enabling the counselor to better profile the one whom God has sent.

THE RESULTS

GOD COUNSELING ADAM AND THE WOMAN (Genesis 3:8-13).

The result of profiling here is that God draws up a profile of Adam and the woman that instantly reveals their condition.

JOSEPH COUNSELING PHARAOH'S CUPBEARER AND BAKER (Genesis 40:6-9).

The result of profiling here is that Joseph is supplied with accurate information by which he is enabled to interpret the dreams.

DANIEL'S COUNSELING OF NEBUCHADNEZZAR (Daniel 4:8-10a)

The result of profiling here is that Daniel is given the facts of the King's dream and is thus able to proceed with the interpretation.

JESUS COUNSELING THE RICH YOUNG MAN (Matthew 19:16-20)

The result of profiling here is that Jesus reveals the real character of the man.

PREMIER CASE STUDY

NATHAN COUNSELS DAVID (II Samuel 12:1)

The result of profiling here is that God had enabled Nathan to proceed counseling David without fear of being misdirected.

In each case, the results of profiling enabled the counselor and the counselee to proceed with accurate and adequate information related to the specific situation. Also, in each case, successful profiling led directly into Step Two of Biblical Directionism counseling --- Comparative Silhouetting.

To initiate the giving of counsel without first having examined, tested, and thus arrived at a determinative profile of the counselee, is to violate a basic premise of sound reasoning.

"A simple man believes anything, but a prudent man gives thought to his steps." Proverbs 14:15.

"He who answers before listening --- that is his folly and his shame." Proverbs 18:13.

"The heart of the discerning acquires knowledge; the ears of the wise seek it out." Proverbs 18:15.

CHAPTER III

QUESTIONS FOR REVIEW

1 Using about 300 words, Explain why "DETERMINATIVE PROFILING" is the initial step of Biblical Directionism, and what means may be generally employed in the process of Determinative Profiling.

_____

_____

2 According to the author, what word is a synonym for "profiling"?

_____

_____

3 According to the author, what is meant by the following statement: "The process of profiling is actually a tripartite event."

_____

_____

4 Using the "Biblical Case Studies" in Chapter Three as a guide, select any biblical event (other than those used in this chapter), which demonstrates "Determinative Profiling". Relate the entire event exactly as it is given in the Scripture. Point out which verses demonstrate profiling.

_____

_____

5 Ideally, what should be the results of Determinative Profiling?

_____

_____

CHAPTER IV

BIBLICAL DIRECTIONISM COUNSELING
STEP TWO:
COMPARATIVE SILHOUETTING

IN THE CONTEXT OF THIS PROCEDURE, a "silhouette" is defined as, "the outline of a body viewed as circumscribing a mass." Thus, "silhouetting" is defined as, "to represent by a silhouette; also: to project on a background like a silhouette." (Webster's Ninth New Collegiate Dictionary.)

In this context, silhouetting is actually two-fold, and referred to as "Comparative Silhouetting." As the second step of Biblical Directionism Counseling, it is that process whereby the results of Determinative Profiling (Step One) are placed into a complete outline form, thereby enabling the counselor to view the individual as a circumscribed whole. This circumscribed whole (the silhouette of the counselee) is then projected "comparatively" on a background silhouette. The background silhouette is always the infallible standard of God's Word, the Bible.

When a silhouette of the counselee's present state of being is placed in a comparative manner upon the background silhouette of Scripture, a revealing comparative outline is projected. This revealing comparative outline is possible because projecting the silhouette of the counselee upon the silhouetted standard of God's Word is actually the process of comparing silhouette with silhouette. That is, the silhouette of the counselee over against the silhouette of the absolutes of the Word of God.

Graphically, this process may be represented as follows:

Silhouette 1a
Represents the Counselee's present state of being

Silhouette 2a
Represents the Standard of God's Word

For a very basic comparison, we may understand the Figures 1a & 2a, and the shapes, as representing data. In the case of Figure 1a, the data suggested by the shape are the identifiable directions of the counselee's current state of being. In the case of Figure 2a, the data suggested by the shape are the identifiable directions of the standards of God's Word for any given situation. Comparative Silhouetting can then be accomplished by contrasting the counselee's silhouette

(Figure 1a), with the biblical silhouette (Figure 2a). This can be graphically represented as follows:

Figures 1a & 2a compared.

Notice the background shape (Figure 2a) represents the silhouette of the standards of God's Word. The foreground shape (Figure 1a) represents the silhouette of the counselee's present state of being. As a result of this comparison, it is easy to determine at what point(s) the counselee is out of alignment with the standards of God's Word.

As a result of this comparative silhouetting, the data gathered as a result of profiling are processed into information. This information becomes the basis for counseling. Where the information assures congruence with the standards of God's Word, the counselee is *not* experiencing a life-problem. Where the information points to incongruence with the standard of God's Word, the counselee *is* experiencing a life-problem.

It is important to point out that the graphic representation of the process of comparative silhouetting is only for illustration. Any number or variety of shapes or images might be used to demonstrate the counselee's condition. What must be understood is that comparative silhouetting is an actual event (process).

The process of comparative silhouetting is essentially that of an analysis between the circumscribed whole of the Scriptural standards which apply to any given situation, and the circumscribed whole of the counselee in his/her current state of being.

Comparative Silhouetting may not always involve the counselee directly. Primarily, the process of Comparative Silhouetting is an intermediate step essential to accurate and viable diagnosis. Consequently, it is an information generating process primarily for the benefit of the counselor.

However, it is often difficult, and sometimes impossible, to exclude the counselee from this process. Neither is it always desirable. For example, silhouetting may be an almost simultaneous process along with profiling, as in the case of a Christian who, in revealing his present problem, already knows whether or not his actions are acceptable according to the biblical norm for his particular situation.

The acceptance of Comparative Silhouetting as the second step in Biblical Directionism Counseling is based upon the belief that God's Word is the infallible absolute in all matters pertaining to human activity; and only by Comparative Silhouetting is the biblical counselor able to reveal and realize the true condition of the counselee.

SCRIPTURAL METHODOLOGY

The single most important factor which characterizes Biblical Directionism counseling, is that fundamental to all counseling, is the belief that the Bible represents an infallible absolute designed to govern and guide the affairs of men. Let it be reasserted, that the Scriptures are quite literally the **RATIONE ET VIA CERTUS**. As such, the Scriptures provide an infallible standard by which man's state of being may be measured.

Just as Determinative Profiling provides a silhouette of the counselee's state of being, so too, the Scriptures provide a silhouette of the norm upon which man's state of being may be contrasted for comparison.

The Scriptural premise from which this second step is derived is found in the Book of Hebrews.

> *"For the Word of God is living and active,*
> *sharper than any double-edged sword, it*
> *penetrates even to dividing soul, spirit,*
> *joints, and marrow it judges the thoughts*
> *and the attitudes of the heart."*
> Hebrews 4:12.

The Scriptures provide a sharp silhouette upon which a person's life may be projected. This silhouette, like that of the counselee's circumscribed whole, is actually "living and active." When the counselee's silhouette is projected upon it for comparison, there is an immediate "penetration" and "dividing" right down to the "thoughts and attitudes of the heart." The result of this process is a "judging" whereby the individual is given a comparative analysis of his or her condition whether for good or for bad.

The Greek word translated "judges" in the NIV is translated "discerner" in the KJV. The word here is "*kritikos.*" The word carries on the thought of "dividing," from "*krinein,*" which means to "divide or separate," which then runs into the sense of "judge," the usual meaning of it in the New Testament. Here, "judgment" involves the sifting out and analysis of evidence. In "*kritikos,*" the ideas of discrimination and judging are blended.

Thus, the Scriptures act as an agent for comparison of the data gathered in profiling. Stated yet another way, it can be said that the Scriptures provide the standard by which an individual's state of being may be contrasted according to an absolute standard.

WHY GOD MUST IMPOSE AN ABSOLUTE STANDARD

Any system of measurement requires a standard. For example, distance may be accurately measured only by reason of an established standard. So, conduct, lifestyle, attitude, thought, action, and reaction, may be measured only in light of an established standard. Insanity, for example, can be measured only on the basis of what standard constitutes sanity.

Biblical Directionism counseling maintains that the standard by which human activity (mental or physical) is measured must transcend mere societal norms. Since societal norms can never be standardized, conduct deemed normal in one element of society may be deemed quite abnormal in another. That societal norms undergo cyclical convolutions is well established. These cyclical convolutions-the changing "ins" and "outs" of what is generally acceptable in any given society-prevent the formulation of any absolute societal standard whereby man's state of being may be properly judged.

It follows that any standard which would serve as an absolute whereby man's state of being can be properly analyzed, would of necessity be required to transcend anything man can design. This concept is germane to the philosophy of Biblical Directionism counseling. Therefore, the Scriptures become the *only* sure standard whereby man's state of being may be assessed, analyzed, and thereby judged.

Without the establishment of a universal transcendental standard, God's will and way for mankind would be subject to the same cyclical uncertainties as societal norms. The resulting confusion would render real sanity impossible and any protective balance in society unattainable. Thus, God has provided an absolute set of standards in His written Word, the Bible.

HOW GOD IMPOSES HIS STANDARD

The word "imposes" is defined as, "to establish or apply by authority." God's absolute standard is established and applied by the authority of His universally distributed laws. One cannot escape the reality of God's righteous requirements.

As an ancient maxim suggests, it is an unchangeable law of God that those who are content with anything less than what they know to be right in the sight of God will sooner or later come to ruin. It is only a matter of time. Genuine fulfillment in this life can only be achieved in humble partnership with the Creator, as one willingly subordinates his or her life to God's control. Or, as the Scriptures say:

> "*Do not be deceived: God cannot be mocked. A man reaps what he sows. The one who sows to please his sinful nature will reap destruction; the one who sows to please the Spirit, from the Spirit will reap eternal life.*" Galatians 6:7-8.

In whatever time/space relationship man happens to find himself, he will also find that living according to the absolute standards of God's Word works toward wholeness, while living in defiance of God's absolute standards works toward fragmentation of his life and relationships.

The transcendental nature of God's standard and its universality, requires its establishment and application to all people of all ages. Hence, when the silhouette of man's circumscribed whole is projected upon the silhouette of God's absolute standards, a realistic lifestyle evidence for comparison is to be expected.

EXPERIENTAL METHODOLOGY

If Comparative Silhouetting is a generic second step in biblical counseling, the Scriptures ought to abound with clear evidence of it. The following selections are only representative of a vast quantity of such evidence, but they do provide realistic and concrete examples.

BIBLICAL CASE STUDIES

GOD COUNSELS CAIN

> *"But Abel brought fat portions from some of the firstborn of his flock. The Lord looked with favor on Abel and his offering, but on Cain and his offering He did not look with favor. So Cain was very angry, and his face was downcast. Then the Lord said to Cain, 'Why are you angry? Why is your face downcast? **If you do what is right, will you not be accepted? But if you do not do what is right, sin is crouching at your door**; it desires to have you, but you must master it.'" Genesis 4:4-7*

God began the conversation with Cain by profiling. "Why are you angry?" "Why is your face downcast?" Next, God compared Cain's silhouette over against His own righteous standard. "If you do what is right, will you not be accepted (God's righteous standard)? But if you do not do what is right, sin is crouching at your door" (Cain's present state of being). A proper comparison has now been drawn between God's silhouette of righteousness and Cain's silhouette (present state of being) or unrighteousness.

REUBEN COUNSELS HIS BROTHERS

*"'Here comes the dreamer!' they said to each other. 'Come now, let's kill him and throw him into one of these cisterns and say that a ferocious animal devoured him. Then we'll see what comes of his dreams.' When Reuben heard this, he tried to rescue him from their hands. 'Let's not take his life,' he said. **Don't shed innocent blood.** Throw him into this cistern here in the desert, but don't lay a hand on him.'"* Genesis 37:19-22a

Reuben is actually silhouetting the heinous intentions of his brothers upon the righteous requirements of God's law --- 'Don't shed any innocent blood" vs22. The silhouette of the brothers is projected upon the standard of God's higher law that prohibited the shedding of innocent blood. This very concept was later incorporated into Mosaic law (Deuteronomy 19:10, 13; 21:8-9; 27:25).

THE PSALMIST'S USE OF SILHOUETTING

"How can a young man keep his way pure? *By living according to Your Word. I seek you with all my heart; do not let me stray from Your commands. I have hid Your Word in my heart that I might not sin against You."* Psalm 119:9-11

Here, the young man is kept pure by a continual process of projecting the circumscribed whole of his life over against that of the silhouette of God's righteous standard: When the two match up, the young man's way is pure.

PETER COUNSELS SIMON THE SORCERER

*"When Simon saw that the Spirit was given at the laying on of the Apostle's hands, he offered them money and said, 'Give me also this ability so that everyone on whom I lay my hands may receive the Holy Spirit.' Peter answered him, 'May your money perish with you, **because you thought you could buy the gift of God with money!** You have no part or share in this ministry, **because your heart is not right before God.'"***
Acts 8:18-21.

Peter, quite openly and publicly, silhouetted Simon's wrong attitude toward the giving of the gift of the Holy Spirit with that of God's standard --- "You thought you could buy the gift of God with money vs20 ... your heart is not right before God" vs21.

PREMIER CASE STUDY

NATHAN COUNSELS DAVID

"The Lord sent Nathan to David. When he came to him, he said, 'There were two men in a certain town, one rich and the other poor. The rich man had a very large number of sheep and cattle, but the poor man had nothing except one little ewe lamb he had bought. He raised it, and it grew up with him and his children. It shared his food, drank from his cup, and even slept in his arms. It was like a daughter to him. Now a traveler came to the rich man, but the rich man refrained from taking one of his own sheep or cattle to prepare a meal for the traveler who had come to him. Instead, he took the ewe lamb that belonged to the poor man and

> *prepared it for the one who had come to him.' David burned with anger against the man and said to Nathan, 'As surely as the Lord lives, the man who did this deserves to die! He must pay for that lamb four times over, because he did such a thing and had no pity.'"*
> II Samuel 12:1-6

In an allegory, Nathan contrasted the actions of the supposed rich neighbor (actually, David himself) over against the righteous standard of God's law.

THE RESULTS

GOD COUNSELS CAIN (Genesis 4:4-7).

The result of Comparative Silhouetting here is that Cain's immediate condition is contrasted in such a way as to reveal the reason for his "anger" and "downcast" face.

REUBEN COUNSELS HIS BROTHERS (Genesis 37:19-22a)

The result of Comparative Silhouetting here is that the proposed action of Reuben's brothers is revealed to be incongruent with God's righteous standard.

THE PSALMIST'S USE OF SILHOUETTING (Psalm 119:9-11)

The result of Comparative Silhouetting here is that the young man is permitted to know the actual standard by which he ought to live. Present actions or attitudes are kept in constant balance with God's Word by reason of a daily routine analysis.

PETER COUNSELS SIMON THE SORCERER (Acts 8:18-21).

The result of Comparative Silhouetting here is that Peter is able to reveal the real motive of Simon by reason of an accurate comparison of God's standard for receiving the gift of the Holy Spirit and Simon's own evil intentions.

PREMIER CASE STUDY

NATHAN COUNSELS DAVID (II Samuel 12:1-6)

The result of Comparative Silhouetting here is sharply defined. David is so incensed at the wickedness of the rich neighbor he "burned with anger" and said, "As surely as the Lord lives, the man who did this deserves to die! He must pay for that lamb four times over, because he did such a thing and had no pity" vs5-6.

David is reflecting back upon the Mosaic law of restitution for sheep stealing which required that four sheep be paid back for every one sheep stolen (Exodus 22:1), and determines the rich neighbor's actions to be unacceptable and wholly evil.

In each case, the results of silhouetting enabled the counselor (and in some cases the counselee) to establish a standard for right and wrong conduct based upon the comparative analysis of the silhouette of man's present state of being, projected upon the silhouette of God's absolute standard.

Attempting to judge actions as right or wrong without some system of infallible absolutes, is to violate the simple and basic premise of sound reason. If no infallible standard exists, then Comparative Silhouetting is only an exercise in futility, and no valid analysis of action or attitude is possible.

> *"For these commands are a lamp, this teaching is a light, and the corrections of discipline are the way to life."*
> Proverbs 6:23.

"So then, the law is holy, and the commandment is holy, righteous and good." Romans 7:12.

CHAPTER IV

QUESTIONS FOR REVIEW

1 Design your own graphic representation of the process of "**COMPARATIVE SILHOUETTING**" as defined in this chapter.

_____
_____
_____
_____

2 Essentially, how can the process of Comparative Silhouetting be defined?

_____
_____
_____

3 Using not less than 250 words, explain why God must impose an absolute standard.

_____
_____
_____

4 Using the case studies in Chapter IV as a guide, select any other biblical event in which the process of Comparative Silhouetting is used. Cite the entire passage. Indicate the portion dealing with silhouetting.

_____
_____
_____
_____

CHAPTER V

BIBLICAL DIRECTIONISM COUNSELING
STEP THREE:
REDEMPTIVE CONFRONTATION

IN THE CONTEXT OF THIS PROCEDURE, "confront" is defined as: "to cause to meet: bring face to face." WEBSTER'S NINTH NEW COLLEGIATE DICTIONARY.

Redemptive Confrontation, as the third step of Biblical Directionism counseling, is the natural concomitant (sequentially) to Determinative Profiling and Comparative Silhouetting. First, the counselee's profile is developed to the point where an accurate silhouette is projected comparatively upon the silhouette of a particular biblical standard. From these two steps, the counselor is able to reach certain viable conclusions regarding the counselee's state of being. Quite logically, the third step involves the need to confront the counselee with these conclusions; that is, bring him or her face to face with the results of the comparative analysis between who, what, and where the infallible standard of God's Word declares he or she ought to be.

Redemptive Confrontation is often difficult and disagreeable. People are not always prepared to accept responsibility for their actions, or to be told certain lifestyle elements are destructive. Here is where discretion, tact, and professionalism are essential. Simply knowing the truth of a given situation is not a license for unbridled brashness. The biblical witness at this point is found in Ephesians 4:15 --- "*Instead, speaking the truth in love, we will in all things grow up into Him Who is the head, that is, Christ.*" A counselor's love for his client ought to compel him to confront, but to do so in love and with the mind of Christ.

The methods employed in Redemptive Confrontation vary and are open to adaptation according to the individual situation. Essentially, Redemptive Confrontation is revealing to the counselee the reality of his or her situation as it is reflected back to them from God's Word. Eventually, however, the time comes when the counselor makes it unequivocally clear to the counselee that certain facts exist in relation to his or her situation. He must bring the counselee face to face with what the standard God's Word reveals.

The acceptance of Redemptive Confrontation as the third and logically sequential third step in Biblical Directionism counseling is based upon the belief that God desires for men and women to know the reasons for their condition, whatever those reasons might happen to be.

SCRIPTURAL METHODOLOGY

Essential to change is the ability and opportunity to know why change is necessary. Without confrontation, such an opportunity does not exist.

The Scriptural premise from which this third step is derived is found in the Book of Ezekiel.

> "*Will you judge them? Then confront them...and say to them: 'This is what the Sovereign Lord says.'*" Ezekiel 20:4-5.

The Hebrew word translated "judge" in the NIV is "*shapat*"; and, in this context, seems to convey a sense of passing judgment or condemning. The Hebrew word translated "confront" in the NIV is translated "cause them to know" in the KJV. The word represented here is, "*yada*" meaning, in this context, "a knowledge of one's relation to the divine."

Consequently, "judging" and "confronting" are related in that a particular decision is reached on the part of the one judging, and the one upon whom that decision is passed is brought face to face with whatever that decision is.

As Confrontation relates to the third step of Biblical Directionism counseling, it is simply bringing the counselee face to face with what he or she really needs to know regarding his or her relationship to the divine, namely, God's infallible absolutes.

WHY GOD MUST CONFRONT MANKIND

The need for Confrontation arises primarily out of the universally sinful condition of man's heart and mind. Being opposed to the things of God, man is naturally prone to wandering from righteousness, justice, and wholeness. Unless confronted with his condition, man remains unrestrained and unrelenting in his quest for carnal satisfaction and self-assertiveness. Confrontation is essential for choice, and choice is essential for change. God, in his love and predestination, has elected that man will be free to make certain spiritual and moral choices. This is the reason for man's capacity for change. But, man is seemingly unable to choose until he is confronted with the options of choice and unable to change if not confronted. This, is why God's confrontation is always redemptive in nature. God never points man to the source of his problem without also directing him toward a solution. God confronts in order to redeem.

The redemptive nature of God's confrontation is both the foundation for, and purpose of, confrontation in Biblical Directionism counseling. Therefore, biblically oriented confrontation must only be understood as redemptive in nature and it is always "Redemptive Confrontation."

That people will not change (for the better), unless confronted, is succinctly testified to in the account of David's wicked son Adonijah. Of Adonijah's wickedness the Scripture says, "His father had never interfered with him by asking, 'Why do you behave as you do?'" I Kings 1:6. David's failure to confront Adonijah resulted in a son who eventually disgraced his family and died at the hand of his brother Solomon; had David loved Adonijah as God loved David, Adonijah would have been confronted and might possibly have chosen to change for the better. Because God loves us, it is His will to redeem us. Therefore, He confronts us.

HOW GOD CONFRONTS MANKIND

As stated previously, the process of confrontation is not exclusively the work of the human counselor. In fact, God has ordained a variety of methods by which men and women may be confronted with the truth. The following examples cover the general scope of God's confrontational methods.

A. Divine Intervention.
(God Himself speaking) Psalm 139:1-24

B. The Written Word.
(The Bible) Hebrews 4:12

C. The Living Word.
(Jesus Christ) John 1:1-5

D. The Other Counselor.
(The Holy Spirit) John 16:5-15

E. Human Instrumentality.
(Counselors, teachers, preachers, etc.)
Ephesians 4:11-13

F. Individual God-consciousness.
(Conviction by reason of conscience)
Romans 1:18-20

Even though God has and does employ a variety of methods whereby He confronts mankind, it pleases Him to make use of human assistants in connection with His healing systems. How God accomplishes this is clearly documented in Scripture.

EXPERIENTIAL METHODOLOGY

If Confrontation is the generic third step in biblical counseling, the Scriptures should abound with clear evidence of it. The following selections are only representative of a vast quantity of such evidence.

BIBLICAL CASE STUDIES

THE ANGEL OF THE LORD COUNSELS BALAAM

> *"The angel of the Lord asked him, 'Why have you beaten your donkey these three times?* **I have come here to oppose you because your path is a reckless one before me. The donkey saw me and turned away from me these three times. If she had not turned away, I would certainly have killed you by now, but I would have spared her.'"***
> Numbers 22:32-33

This case is quite clear. Balaam's donkey prevented Balaam's death, and the Angel of the Lord confronted Balaam with the facts of his near death and the reason why.

Joshua counsels the nation of Israel

*"Joshua said to the people, 'You are not able to serve the Lord. He is a Holy God; He is a jealous God. He will not forgive your rebellion and your sins. **If you forsake the Lord and serve foreign gods, He will turn and bring disaster on you, and make an end of you, after He has been good to you.'** But the people said to Joshua, 'No! We will serve the Lord.'"* Joshua 24:19-24

After properly profiling and silhouetting the condition of the nation of Israel, Joshua confronted them with the facts of their present state of being.

Deborah counsels Barak

*"Barak said to her, 'If you go with me, I will go; but if you don't go with me, I won't go.' 'Very well,' Deborah said, 'I will go with you. **But because of the way you are going about this, the honor will not be yours**, for the Lord will hand Sisera over to a woman.' So Deborah went with Barak to Kedesh."* Judges 4:8-9

Having explained to Barak God's plan for the deliverance of Israel out of the hands of Jabin, the Canaanite king, Deborah was faced with Barak's hesitation. Deborah confronted Barak with the consequences of his decision.

Peter counsels Ananias and Sapphira

*"Then Peter said, **'Ananias, how is it that Satan has so filled your heart***

> *that you have lied to the Holy Spirit
> and have kept for yourself some of
> the money you received for the land?
> Didn't it belong to you before it was
> sold? And after it was sold, wasn't
> the money at your disposal? What
> made you think of doing such a
> thing? You have not lied to men but to
> God.'* When Ananias heard this, he fell
> down and died. And great fear seized all
> who heard what had happened."
> Acts 5:3-5

In this terrifying account of rebellion against God's
standard of righteousness, Peter confronted Ananias
(and later his wife, Sapphira) with the consequence of
his violation.

PREMIER CASE STUDY

NATHAN COUNSELS DAVID

> *"Then Nathan said to David, 'You are
> the man!'"* II Samuel 12:7a

Nathan had received an exact profile of
David from God. He skillfully silhouetted
David's past action by the use of a
parable and now confronted David with
the seriousness of his transgression.

THE RESULTS

THE ANGEL OF THE LORD COUNSELS BALAAM
(Numbers 22:32-33)

The result of confrontation here is that Balaam is
brought face to face with how close he had come to
death and why he had been spared.

JOSHUA COUNSELS THE NATION OF ISRAEL (Joshua 24:19-20)

The result of confrontation here is that the nation of Israel was faced with the reality of their condition, being made aware that a choice must be made and what they can expect as a result of such a choice.

DEBORAH COUNSELS BARAK (Judges 4:8-9)

The result of confrontation here is that Barak was brought face to face with the consequences of his fearful hesitation and lack of faith in God's plan.

PETER COUNSELS ANANIAS AND SAPPHIRA (Acts 5:3-5)

The result of confrontation here are graphic and terrifying. Both Ananias and his wife die instantly of the shock of the confrontation. This narrative serves as an example and unsettling reminder that confrontation may not always result in an opportunity for which to change. There may be actions against God's standards that are irrevocable. There may be times when confrontation only brings the individual face to face with severe consequences for which forgiveness alone may be the answer.

PREMIER CASE STUDY

NATHAN COUNSELS DAVID (II Samuel 12:7)

The result of confrontation here is to bring David face to face with the fact that neither God or man had whitewashed the king's awful atrocity against Uriah. And in this case, there would be a high price to pay along with the need for a decision of great importance. In each case, the results of confrontation involved the explanation of how the counselee's present state of being was the result of a failure to have acted in accordance with the standard of God's word. It also involved pointing out what was to be expected as a result of the current condition.

Attempting to assist an individual through counseling, without arriving at the proper point in time to a moment of confrontation, is to violate a simple and basic premise of sound reason. If Confrontation is given no place in the counseling process, how is one to determine the nature of past actions, their possible consequences, and the possibility of corrective actions?

> *"What will I do when God confronts me? What will I answer when called to account?"* Job 31:14

> *"Search me, O God, and know my heart; test me and know my anxious thoughts. See if there is any offensive way in me, and lead me in the way everlasting."* Psalm 139:23-24

> *"A fool spurns his father's discipline, but whoever heeds correction shows prudence."* Proverbs 15:5

> *"Then Samuel said to the people, 'It is the Lord who appointed Moses and Aaron and brought your forefathers up out of Egypt. Now then, stand here, because I am going to confront you with evidence before the Lord as to all the righteous acts performed by the Lord for you and your fathers.'"* I Samuel 12:6-7

CHAPTER V

QUESTIONS FOR REVIEW

1 Why is "**REDEMPTIVE CONFRONTATION**" dependent upon the first two (2) steps of Directionism?

_____
_____
_____
_____
_____

2 Why is Confrontation essential to change?

_____
_____
_____
_____
_____

3 Using not more than 200 words, explain why God must confront mankind.

_____
_____
_____
_____
_____

4 Using the biblical case studies contained in Chapter V as a guide, locate one other biblical example of Redemptive Confrontation. Indicate the portion dealing with Confrontation.

_____
_____
_____
_____
_____

CHAPTER VI

BIBLICAL DIRECTIONISM COUNSELING
STEP FOOUR:
INDIVIDUAL COMMITMENT

IN THE CONTEXT OF THIS PROCEDURE, "commit" is defined as: "to carry into action deliberately." Thus, "commitment" is defined as: 'the state of being obligated or emotionally impelled." (WEBSTER'S NINTH NEW COLLEGIATE DICTIONARY.)

Individual Commitment, as the fourth step of Biblical Directionism counseling, is the naturally sequential step following Redemptive Confrontation (Step Three). After Redemptive Confrontation (where the counselee is brought face to face with the conditions and consequences of his or her present state of being), a decision must be made to deliberately act upon the biblical criteria for redemptive change. That is, the counselee must decide to carry into action the biblical solutions *necessary* for redemptive change.

Individual Commitment is the fourth step of Biblical Directionism counseling when the counselor assists the counselee in deliberately agreeing to enter a state of obligation to the corrective action necessary for healing. This state of obligation ought to serve as both an intellectual and emotional facilitator which motivates the counselee toward commitment to change. Stated perhaps more succinctly, individual commitment involves bringing the counselee face to face with the need to make a commitment to follow the biblical direction necessary for help and healing.

The acknowledgement of individual commitment as the fourth and logically sequential step following confrontation, is based upon the belief that God requires from man an individual and deliberate decision to carry into action the truth of His Word if genuine restoration is to be realized.

SCRIPTURAL METHODOLOGY

Essential to real restoration, is the willingness on the part of the counselee to actually adopt a therapeutic regime. Resistance to change and reluctance to cooperate with known and proven methods of therapy are universally recognized as the primary barriers to successful counseling. That help is available for any given situation is a biblical absolute; that such help is available only if sought and appropriated is likewise a biblical absolute.

The Scriptural premise from which this fourth step is derived is found in the Book of Matthew.

> *"Come unto Me all you who are weary and burdened, and I will give you rest. Take My yoke upon you and learn of Me, for I am gentle and humble in heart and you will find rest for your souls. For My yoke is easy and My burden is light."*
> Matthew 11:28-30

The offer for help is explicit in the words, "come, take, learn." These three proffered invitations for help and healing carry an implicit demand for personal acceptance and individual accountability.

The Greek word translated "come" is *"deute"* and is the plural of *"deuro"* which means "come here." It is actually a call designed to incite the hearer with an imperative to come. That this word is in the plural implies the universality of the call to come. The Greek word translated "take" is *"arate"* which means "to take up, lift, rise." There is conveyed in this word the idea of active participation on the part of the one called to take.

The Greek word translated "learn" is "*mathete*" which means "to increase one's knowledge, or be increased in knowledge, frequently to learn by inquiry or observation." Implicit here is active participation in the learning process on the part of the individual learner.

Inherent in Jesus' call to "come, take, learn" is the concept of commitment. One is called to actually come, take up, and begin to learn. A deliberate decision to take action is essential. Notice that the acts of coming, taking up, and learning must, by the nature of them involve an individual's willing participation.

The rewards of commitment are explicit:
1. there is the promise of rest from the burden;

2. an easy yoke (a yoke being an instrument used to ease the burden of carrying heavy loads);

3. a lighter load (easier burden);

4. the lessons of a gentle and humble mind (heart);

5. rest for the soul.

All these rewards are only possible as a consequence of commitment to the call. This principle is not exclusive to Biblical Directionism counseling or even to God's dealings with man. It is inherent in a great many systems. However, it is perhaps more obvious in counseling systems; for, in any counseling model, Individual Commitment is essential to meaningful results.

WHY GOD REQUIRES COMMITMENT

In Psalm 37:5, David said, "*Commit your way to the Lord; trust in Him and He will do this: He will make your righteousness shine like the dawn, the justice of your cause like the noon day sun.*" The Hebrew word translated "commit" is "*galal*" which means "to roll." Thus, to "commit" one's life unto the Lord is to "roll" it upon Him. Implicit in the idea of "rolling upon" is the necessity of deliberate and decisive action which is prompted or motivated by personal willingness to accept both the liberty and constraint of turning one's way over to God.

A righteous God must require commitment of those who would be the recipients of His healing systems. Otherwise, there must be universal healing for every wrong thing regardless of individual accountability. If such were the case, no system of absolutes could be possible; and without His system of absolutes, God would not be God.

This same principle is established within a great many secular disciplines and societal systems. Jurisprudence, for example, deteriorates into a meaningless exercise in irrelevant philosophy if the element of personal responsibility is removed. Are God's righteous requirements to be taken less seriously than the state-established requirements of law? And what system of counseling (secular or biblical) could possibly be effective without the all-important element of Individual Commitment? The primary factor in counseling success/failure for all types of methodologies is the degree of Individual Commitment on the part of the counselee.

God requires Individual Commitment because He has established that, for the duration of earth-life, mankind will be free to commit to the righteous requirements of the ways of God or be free to reject them. Thus, individual commitment is an irrevocable prerequisite to healing.

HOW GOD REQUIRES COMMITMENT

The manner in which God requires commitment is three-fold. First, God requires **REPENTANCE** for past actions and attitudes that were incongruent with righteousness (right living and right thinking) (Luke 13:1-5; II Peter 3:9). Second, God requires **RESTITUTION** for wrongs committed against others (wherever this is possible) (Exodus 22:3-14; Leviticus 5:16; 6:5; 22:14; 24:18-21; Numbers 5:8). Third, God requires **REALIGNMENT** of attitudes and actions according to the infallible standards of His Word (right living and right thinking) (Micah 6:8; Hebrews 12:14).

Perhaps no other passage of Scripture teaches this lesson quite as succinctly as Isaiah 1:16-20.

> *"Wash and make yourselves clean. Take your evil deeds out of My sight! Stop doing wrong, learn to do right! Seek justice, encourage the oppressed. Defend the cause of the fatherless, plead the cause of the widow. 'Come now, let us reason together,' says the Lord. 'Though your sins are like scarlet, they shall be as white as snow; though they are red as crimson, they shall be like wool. If you are willing and obedient, you will eat the best from the land; but if you resist and rebel, you will be devoured by the sword.' For the mouth of the Lord has spoken."*

EXPERIENTIAL METHODOLOGY

If Commitment is to be the generic fourth step in biblical counseling, the Scriptures should abound with clear evidence of it. The following selections are only representative of a vast quantity of such evidence.

Biblical Case Studies

God counsels Noah

*"So God said to Noah, 'I am going to put an end to all people, for the earth is filled with violence because of them. I am surely going to destroy both them and the earth. **So make yourself an ark of cypress wood; make rooms in it and coat it with pitch inside and out. This is how you are to build it**:'...Noah did everything just as God commanded him."* Genesis 6:13-15a, 22.

That Commitment was required is clearly shown in the words, "So make yourself an ark." vs14; "This is how you are to build it:" vs15.

Jethro counsels Moses

*"Moses' father-in-law replied, 'What you are doing is not good. You and these people who come to you will only wear yourselves out. This work is too heavy for you; you cannot handle it alone. **Listen now to me and I will give you some advice, and may God be with you**'...Moses listened to his father-in-law and did everything he said."* Exodus 18:17-19a, 24.

That Commitment was required here is clearly shown in the words, "Listen now to me and I will give you some advise" vs19.

Eli counsels Samuel

*"So Eli told Samuel, '**Go and lie down,**

> **and if He calls you, say, Speak, Lord,
> for your servant is listening.**' *So
> Samuel went and lay down in his place.
> The Lord came and stood there, calling as
> at the other times, 'Samuel! Samuel!'
> Then Samuel said, 'Speak, for your
> servant is listening.'"* I Samuel 3:9-10

That Commitment was required here is demonstrated in
the words, "Go and lie down, and if He calls you, say,
'Speak, Lord, for your servant is listening'" vs9.

JESUS COUNSELS SIMON

> *"When He had finished speaking, He said
> to Simon, **'Put out into deep water,
> and let down the nets for a catch.'**
> Simon answered, 'Master, we've worked
> hard all night and haven't caught
> anything. But because You say so, I will
> let down the nets.' When they had done
> so, they caught such a large number of
> fish that their nets began to break."*
> Luke 5:4-6.

That Commitment was required here is show by
the argument Simon puts up about having worked
all night and caught nothing---still Jesus required
commitment..."Put out into deep water, and let down
the nets for a catch" vs4.

PREMIER CASE STUDY

NATHAN COUNSELS DAVID

> *"You did it in secret, but I will do this
> thing in broad daylight before all Israel.'*

> *Then David said to Nathan, 'I have sinned against the Lord.'* Nathan replied, *'The Lord has taken away your sin. You are not going to die.'''* II Samuel 12:12-13

That Commitment was required here is demonstrated in David's reaction to Nathan's confrontation..."I have sinned against the Lord" vs13. The essential and initial step of commitment is **REPENTANCE**; this, David knew full well and willingly took this step as an evidence of his deliberate decision to take whatever action necessary to correct his life.

THE RESULTS

GOD COUNSELS NOAH (Genesis 6:13-15a, 22)

The results of a call to commitment here is revealed in these words, "Noah did everything just as God commanded him" vs22.

Jethro counsels Moses (Exodus 18:17-19, 24)

The result of the call to commitment is revealed in these words, "Moses listened to his father-in-law and did everything he said" vs24.

ELI COUNSELS SAMUEL (I Samuel 3:9-10)

The result of the call to commitment is revealed in these words, "So Samuel went and lay down in his place" vs9; "Then Samuel said, 'Speak, for your servant is listening'" vs5.

PREMIER CASE STUDY

NATHAN COUNSELS DAVID (II Samuel 12:12-13)

The results of David's willing commitment is revealed in the words of David, "I have sinned against the Lord" vs13.

In each of the above case studies, the counselee was faithful to the call for commitment. Certainly, the Scriptures are replete with case studies where the counselee failed to be faithful to the call for commitment. In all such cases, tragedy resulted. Examples include:

a. Cain's rejection of God's call to repentance (Genesis 4);

b. the nation of Israel's rejection of Moses' call to enter the promised land (Numbers 13);

c. Jonah's initial rejection of God's call to go to Nineveh (Jonah 1);

d. the rich young man's rejection of Jesus' call to self-abnegation (Matthew 19).

The contrast between the case studies of those willingly committed and those who refused provides a clear picture of how, without commitment, positive change is impossible.

To confront a counselee with the realities of his or her present state of being without also calling him or her to commitment is to violate the simple and basic premise of sound reasoning.

> *"Many are the woes of the wicked, but the Lord's unfailing love surrounds the man who trusts in Him."* Psalm 32:10.

> *"The Lord redeems His servants; no one who takes refuge in Him will be condemned."* Psalm 34:22.

> *"Fear of man will prove to be a snare, but whoever trusts in the Lord will be kept safe."* Proverbs 29:25.

"Let us, therefore, make every effort to enter that rest, so that no one will fall by following their example of disobedience." Hebrews 4:11.

CHAPTER VI

QUESTIONS FOR REVIEW

1 Give a succinct definition of "INDIVIDUAL COMMITMENT" as the fourth step of Directionism.

_____
_____
_____

2 As the fourth step in Directionism, "INDIVIDUAL COMMITMENT" is based upon what essential belief?

_____
_____
_____

3 Universally, what is the primary barrier to successful counseling? Why?

_____
_____
_____

4 Using not more than 300 words, explain why God requires Individual Commitment.

_____
_____
_____

5 Using the biblical case studies in Chapter Six as a guide, select another biblical example of "INDIVIDUAL COMMITMENT". Cite the entire reference, pointing out the portion dealing with "Commitment."

_____
_____
_____

CHAPTER VII

BIBLICAL DIRECTIONISM COUNSELING
STEP FIVE:
PERSONAL CONDITIONING

IN THE CONTEXT OF THIS PROCEDURE, "Conditioning" is defined as: "to adapt, modify, or mold." (WEBSTER'S NEW COLLEGIATE DICTIONARY.)

Personal Conditioning, as the fifth and final step of Biblical Directionism counseling, has one primary goal: to move the counselee from Individual Commitment (Step Four) to the experiential reality of literal change. That is, Personal Conditioning is designed to implement the adaptation, modification, and molding of the counselee's state of being, whereby he or she is able to bring his or her life into conformity with the principles of God's Word.

Personal Conditioning is viewed as a cooperative agreement between counselor, counselee, and the Holy Spirit, with the burden of proof resting upon the counselee in the matter of actual practice. In this regard, personal conditioning is to be not merely a short-term solution to a long-standing problem but, rather, a life-long process of adapting, modifying, and molding one's life within the framework of the Scriptures.

The *short-term* goal of personal conditioning is immediate adaptation, modification, and molding. The *long-term* goal of personal conditioning is that this process of conditioning will continue life-long but without the continual aid of the counselor. The ultimate goal of Biblical Directionism counseling is to assist the counselee in becoming free from dependency upon counselors and totally dependent upon God and His Word for the direction necessary to live in a state of well-being. Biblical Directionism counseling has as its primary goal the hope of assisting the counselee in becoming Christ-centered and Christ-dependent. This goal can only be fully realized by way of life-long Personal Conditioning.

The methods employed in Personal Conditioning vary and are predicated to some extent upon the specific situation. Personal conditioning may be accomplished by the use of homework assignments, projects of various types, or cooperative arrangements between the counselee and other involved persons. Essential to the success of any Personal Conditioning is the need to make clear to the counselee both the reason *why* a particular adaptation, modification, or molding is required and *how* he or she may actually implement what is required.

The acceptance of personal conditioning as the fifth and final step of Biblical Directionism counseling is based upon the belief that genuine change must be ultimately demonstrated by empirical evidence.

SCRIPTURAL METHODOLOGY

Essential to literal conditioning is the need, on the part of the counselee, to know and understand the reason and the rationale of the biblical principles necessary for positive change. Most especially is this true if the process of Personal Conditioning is to continue life-long. The counselee must develop a system of what may be properly termed "continuing education." It is the goal of Personal Conditioning to initiate both a process of *"immediate"* and *"continuing"* education.

The Scriptural premise upon which this final step is developed is found in the Book of Ezekiel.

> *"They are to teach My people the difference between the holy and the common, and show them how to distinguish between the unclean and the clean."* Ezekiel 44:23

The process of Personal Conditioning, as illustrated in the above text, is two-fold. First, "They are to teach My people the difference between the holy and the common." This corresponds with short-term conditioning whereby the counselor assists the counselee in immediate adaptation, modification, and molding. Second, "show them how to distinguish between the unclean and the clean." This corresponds with the long-term goal of conditioning whereby the counselee becomes skilled at the use of God's Word and is able to make any necessary distinction without the continual need of a human counselor.

The word translated "teach" in the NIV is the Hebrew word "*yara*". "The basic idea of the root '*yara*' is 'to throw' or 'to cast' with the strong sense of control by the subject. The three most frequent uses of this root deal with shooting arrows, sending rain, and teaching." Thus, teaching is an act of "throwing out" or "pointing out." One might correctly restate the verse by translating "*yara*" as such---"They are to *point out* to My people the difference between the holy and the common."

The first part of personal conditioning involves "pointing out" or "teaching" the counselee the course of right action.

The Hebrew word translated "distinguish" in the NIV is translated "discern" in the KJV. The word represented here is "*yada*" meaning, in this context, "to distinguish".

The word "distinguish", as applied here, is defined as "to perceive a difference in: mentally separate."

The second part of Personal Conditioning is to bring the counselee to the place where he or she is personally able to "mentally separate" right attitude and action from wrong attitude and action based upon his or her ability to "distinguish" on the basis of God's Word.

Thus, if the concepts of "teach My people the difference" and "show them how to distinguish" are divided correctly, we see clearly the two-fold application of Personal Conditioning. This two-fold application is the closure point of Biblical Directionism counseling so far as the counselor is concerned, and is totally open-ended so far as the counselee is concerned.

WHY GOD IIMPOSES CONDITIONING

The reason for God's imposition of personal conditioning upon His people is simply that without it man would never move on to corrective action, neither would real spiritual maturaty ever be possible. This principle is clearly illustrated in the following Scriptures.

> "Jesus replied, 'No one who puts his hand
> to the plow and looks back is fit for service
> in the kingdom of God.'" Luke 9:62

> "But now that you know God---or rather
> are known by God--how is it that you are
> turning back to those weak and miserable
> principles? Do you wish to be enslaved by
> them all over again?" Galatians 4:9

> "Therefore let us leave the elementary
> teachings about Christ and go on into
> maturity, not laying again the
> foundation of repentance from acts that

lead to death, and of faith in God, instruction on baptisms, the laying on of hands, the resurrection of the dead, and eternal judgment. And God permitting, we will do so. It is impossible for those who have once been enlightened, who have tasted the heavenly gift, who have shared in the Holy Spirit, and have tasted the goodness of God and the powers of the coming age, if they fall away, to be brought back to repentance, because of their loss they are crucifying the Son of God all over again and subjecting Him to public disgrace." Hebrews 6:1-6

"All Scripture is God-breathed and is useful for teaching, rebuking, correcting and training in righteousness, so that the man of God may be thoroughly equipped for every good work." II Timothy 3:16-17

Failure to move on into Personal Conditioning, whereby one's life is adapted, modified, and molded by the will and way of God is the primary cause of late-phase failure in most counseling cases. The process of Determinative Profiling, Comparative Silhouetting, Redemptive Confrontation, and Individual Commitment may all move effectively. But, failure to go on into Personal Conditioning will always result in the breakdown of the counseling process. Men and women must always be motivated to move forward into the life-long process of Personal Conditioning.

HOW GOD ACCOMPLISHES CONDITIONING

God accomplishes Personal Conditioning in much the same manner as He accomplishes the process of Redemptive Confrontation. Here again, let it be understood that the human counselor is only one of many human and Divine persons used by the Lord in the rehabilitation of His children.

Nevertheless, Personal Conditioning is one of the elements of God's dealings with man whereby the individual (the counselee) must bear the weight of responsibility. Through the written Word, the ministry of the Holy Spirit, and the use of human counselors, God may communicate His will and way; but, in the final analysis, it is the individual's willingness to cooperate that determines the outcome.

Once the individual enters the adaptation, modifying, and molding stage of conditioning, another of God's methods for impelling positive change comes into play. This might be termed the "law of sowing and reaping." This law is well defined in the following text.

> *"Each one should test his own actions. Then he can take pride in himself, without comparing himself to somebody else, for each one should carry his own load. Any one who receives instruction in the Word must share all good things with his instructor. Do not be deceived: God cannot be mocked. A man reaps what he sows. The one who sows to please his sinful nature, from that nature will reap destruction; the one who sows to please the Spirit, from the Spirit will reap eternal life. Let us not become weary in doing good, for at the proper time we will reap a harvest if we do not give up. Therefore, as we have opportunity, let us do good to all people, especially to those who belong to the family of believers."* Galatians 6:4-10

The good harvest of right actions is a powerful influence for continual conditioning. The rewards of adapting, modifying, and molding one's life according to the principles of God's Word are usually sufficient as an inducement to life-long orthopraxies. The wonderful thing about the instruction given in God's Word is that it works exactly as promised!

EXPERIENTIAL METHODOLOGY

If Personal Conditioning is the generic final step in biblical counseling, the Scriptures will abound with clear evidence of it. The following selections are only representative of a vast quantity of such evidence.

BIBLICAL CASE STUDIES

TWO ANGELS COUNSEL LOT AND HIS FAMILY

> *"With the coming of dawn, the angels urged Lot, saying, 'Hurry! Take your wife and your two daughters who are here, or you will be swept away when the city is punished.' When he hesitated, the men grasped his hand and the hands of his wife and of his two daughters and led them safely out of the city, for the Lord was merciful to them. As soon as they had brought them out, one of them said,* **'Flee for your lives! Don't look back, and don't stop anywhere on the plain!** *Flee to the mountains or you will be swept away!' But Lot's wife looked back and she became a pillar of salt."* Genesis 19:15-17, 26

Here, Personal Conditioning is in the form of a specific command, "Flee for your lives! Don't look back, and don't stop anywhere in the plain!" vs17.

NAOMI COUNSELS RUTH

> *"One day Naomi her mother-in-law said to her, 'My daughter, should I not try to find a home for you, where you will be well provided for? Is not Boaz, with whose servant girls you have been, a kinsman of ours? Tonight he will be winnowing barley on the threshing floor.* **Wash and perfume yourself, and put on your best clothes. Then go down to the threshing floor, and don't let him know that you are there until he has finished eating and drinking. When he lies down, note the place where he is lying. Then go and uncover his feet and lie down.** *He will tell you what to do.' 'I will do whatever you say,' Ruth answered. So she went down to the threshing floor and did everything her mother-in-law told her to do. So Boaz took Ruth and she became his wife. And the Lord enabled her to conceive, and she gave birth to a son."*
> Ruth 3:1-6; 4:13

In this case, Personal Conditioning is in the form of a difficult and unusual recommendation. What Naomi asks of her daughter-in-law is so strange that only Ruth's commitment to doing right could have possibly sustained her through the literal implementation.

ELISHA COUNSELS NAAMAN

> *"Elisha sent a messenger to him to say,* **'Go, wash yourself seven times in the Jordan, and your flesh will be restored and you will be cleansed.'** *But Naaman went away angry and said,*

*'I thought that he would surely come out
to me and stand and call on the name of
the Lord his God, wave his hand over the
spot and cure me of my leprosy. Are not
Abana and Pharpar, the rivers of
Damascus, better than any of the waters
of Israel? Couldn't I wash in them and be
cleansed?' So he turned and went off in a
rage. Naaman's servants went to him
and said, 'My father, if the prophet had
told you to do some great thing, would
you not have done it? How much more,
then when he tells you, wash and be
cleansed!' So he went down and dipped
himself in the Jordan seven times, as the
man of God had told him, and his flesh
was restored and became clean like that
of a young boy."* II Kings 5:10-14

The tremendous requirement of humility involved here
at first, became a barrier to Naaman's healing. Personal
conditioning often requires the breaking of the pride
barrier. In this case, Personal Conditioning was
essential, in that only by following Elisha's specific
command, "Go, wash seven times in the Jordan" vs10,
could he be healed.

GOD COUNSELS ANANIAS CONCERNING SAUL

*But the Lord said to Ananias, 'Go! This
man is My chosen instrument to carry My
name before the Gentiles and their kings
and before the people of Israel. I will show
him how much he must suffer for My
name.' Then Ananias went to the house
and entered it. Placing his hands on Saul,
he said, 'Brother Saul, the Lord---Jesus,
Who appeared to you on the road as you
were coming here---has sent me so that*

*you may see again and be filled with the
Holy Spirit.' Immediately, something like
scales fell from Saul's eyes, and he could
see again. He got up and was baptized,
and after taking some food, he regained
his strength."* Acts 9:15-19

God's call to Ananias for Personal Conditioning was not
an easy command to obey. The reputation of Saul was
such that Ananias had good reason to fear for his life.
The biblical call to Personal Conditioning is often a
risky thing by man's standard, and only the genuinely
committed will actually take that step of adaptation,
modifying, and molding.

PREMIER CASE STUDY

NATHAN COUNSELS DAVID

***"But because by doing this you have
made the enemies of the Lord show
utter contempt, the son born to you
will die.'*** *After Nathan had gone home,
the Lord struck the child that Uriah's wife
had borne to David, and he became ill.
David pleaded with God for the child. He
fasted and went into his house and spent
the nights lying on the ground. David
noticed that his servants were whispering
among themselves and he realized the
child was dead. 'Is the child dead?' he
asked. 'Yes,' they replied, 'he is dead.'
Then David got up from the ground.
After he had washed, put on lotions, and
changed his clothes he went in the house
of the Lord and worshiped. Then David
comforted his wife Bathsheba, and he
went to her and lay with her. She gave
birth to a son, and they named him*

Solomon. The Lord loved him; and because the Lord loved him, He sent word through Nathan the prophet to name him Jedidiah." (Note: Jedidiah means loved by the Lord.) II Samuel 12:14-16; 19-20a; 24-25

While the ways of God are always infinitely above the ways of men, this particular account of God's dealing is so extraordinary that it defies full explanation. However, the call to Personal Conditioning is a call to David's heart; that is, a call to remain faithful to God through the pain and embarrassment of public exposure and the death of the son conceived through his adulterous relationship to Bathsheba.

THE RESULTS

TWO ANGELS COUNSEL LOT AND HIS FAMILY (Genesis 19:15-17; 26)

The results of Personal Conditioning here are mixed. Lot and his two daughters are obedient, while Lot's wife failed to adapt. As a result, Lot and his daughters are saved, and his wife is lost. Such is always the result of obedience/disobedience. Those who adapt, modify, and mold their lives to the Personal Conditioning call of God will experience reward. Those who refuse, no matter how well-intentioned, will experience loss.

NAOMI COUNSELS RUTH (Ruth 3:1-6; 4:13)

The result of personal conditioning here is obvious. "So Boaz took Ruth and she became his wife. And the Lord enabled her to conceive, and she gave birth to a son" (4:13).

ELISHA COUNSELS NAAMAN (II Kings 5:10-14)

The results of obedience to Personal Conditioning are clearly expressed in verse 15: "his flesh was restored and became like that of a young man."

GOD COUNSELS ANANIAS CONCERNING SAUL (Acts 9:15-19)

The results of Personal Conditioning here are actually two-fold. Both Ananias and Saul receive the benefits of obedience to God's command. It is most often the case that when any individual remains faithful to the personal conditioning required as a consequence of his or her commitment to God, others will surely benefit also.

PREMIER CASE STUDY

NATHAN COUNSELS DAVID
(II Samuel 12:14-16; 19-20a; 24-25)

For the purpose of recapitulation, all five stages of Nathan's counseling of David will be reviewed here.

> **STEP ONE:** Determinative Profiling (II Samuel 12:1). God revealed to Nathan all the facts concerning David's sin with Bathsheba. Consequently, Nathan is able to proceed with his counseling without fear of misdiagnosis or misdirection.

> **STEP TWO:** Comparative Silhouetting (II Samuel 12:1-6). Nathan took the determinative profile data provided by God and projects compared that data against the righteous standard of God's law. David became so incensed at the injustice of the case that he clearly saw the incongruence between the act committed and the standard violated.

> **STEP THREE:** Redemptive Confrontation (II Samuel 12:7a). Following the clearly defined comparative silhouetting and David's declaration that the man was deserving of punishment, Nathan brought David face to face with the reality of his own sinful condition.

85

STEP FOUR: Individual Commitment (II Samuel 12:12-13). David was king and, as such, was all-powerful in matters of government and law. He might easily have sentenced Nathan to prison or condemned him to be executed. Nathan's confrontation of David required an individual commitment from the King. David must either commit to God's call and repent or commit to rejecting God's call and order Nathan's punishment. That David committed to God's call for repentance is confirmed in his own words, "I have sinned against the Lord" vs13.

STEP FIVE: Personal Conditioning (II Samuel 12:14-16; 19-20a; 24-25). In this final step, the call to Personal Conditioning is expressed in Nathan's warning, "The son born to you will die" vs14. Even after his powerful expression of individual commitment vs13, David might easily have refused to enter this final phase.

However, his willingness to adapt, modify, and mold is implicitly shown in his attitude and actions immediately following Nathan's warning that the son born to Bathsheba would die. This same willingness is explicit in verse twenty. "Then David got up from the ground. After he had washed, put on lotions, and changed his clothes, he went into the house of the Lord and worshiped." The final result of David's willingness to enter conditioning is revealed in verse twenty-four. "Then David comforted his wife, Bathsheba, and he went to her and lay with her. She gave birth to a son,

and they named him Solomon. The Lord
loved him..."

SUMMARY

The Premier Case Study of Nathan's counseling of
David illustrates clearly the relationship each of the five
steps of Biblical Directionism counseling has with the
other. Quite naturally, all five steps tend to interface
with one another and must be viewed with libation
when considering actual implementation. While totally
rigid, sequential implementation will tend to weaken
the system's natural effectiveness, it is equally true that
indiscriminate application of the Five Steps will disrupt
the inherent balance of this methodologically designed
system of biblical counseling.

The Premier Case study also illustrates the fact that
Biblical Directionism counseling is neither a quick or
easy way out of a problem. David and Bathsheba lost
the illegitimate son born of their adulterous union;
David's sin was made known to the nation; and David's
older sons apparently loathed their father from that
time on. Yet, God did forgive and offer a pattern for
recovery. God's ways are not paths of least resistance,
but they are always paths of righteousness, and reward
of righteousness ought to be sufficient inducement for
conditioning one's life according to the Word of God
(Psalm 25:2).

To bring a counselee to a place of commitment then
fail to lead him or her on to actual adaptation,
modification, and molding of his or her state of being
to the infallible standards of God's Word, is to violate
the simple and basic premise of sound reasoning.

> "But solid food is for the mature, who by
> constant use have trained themselves to
> distinguish good and evil." Hebrews 5:14

"For this very reason, make every effort to add to your faith goodness; and to goodness, knowledge; and to knowledge, self-control; and to self-control, perseverance; and to perseverance, godliness; and to godliness, brotherly kindness; and to brotherly kindness, love. For if you possess these qualities in increasing measure, they will keep you from being ineffective and unproductive in your knowledge of our Lord Jesus Christ. But if anyone does not have them, he is nearsighted and blind, and has forgotten that he has been cleansed from his past sins. Therefore, my brother, be all the more eager to make your calling and election sure. For if you do these things, you will never fall, and you will receive a rich welcome into the eternal kingdom of our Lord and Savior Jesus Christ." II Peter 1:5-11

CHAPTER VII

QUESTIONS FOR REVIEW

1 Using not more than 150 words, define the term "**PERSONAL CONDITIONING**" as presented in the text.

_____

_____

_____

2 List the "short-term" and "long-term" goals of Personal Conditioning.

_____

_____

_____

3 What is the "ultimate" goal of Directionism counseling?

_____

_____

_____

4 Using not more than 200 words, explain why God imposes Personal Conditioning.

_____

_____

_____

5 Using the biblical case studies in Chapter Seven as a guide, select another biblical example of "Personal Conditioning." Cite the entire reference, pointing out the portion dealing with Personal Conditioning.

_____

_____

_____

6 Using the "Premier Case Study" as a guide, select any other biblical example which reflects the entire process of Directionism counseling (each of the five steps). Cite the entire reference, pointing out the portions dealing with each of the five (5) steps and summarize the final results of the entire process. **NOTE:** You may select a case which reflects either success or failure.

_____

_____

_____

7 From your own experience and using the five points of Biblical Directionism counseling, create a hypothetical case study. State the presenting problem, and outline how each of the five steps were applied. Suggest the possible results. Use not more than 750 words.

_____

_____

_____

CONCLUSION

In the Introduction, referring to the generic nature of Biblical Directionism Counseling, I stated: "Therefore, it is the goal of this text to present (not invent) this system in such a way as to make it so clear that it becomes obvious that the author is only a student of the Word accepting Biblical basics. Trusting that this goal has been accomplished, I will add only a few concluding thoughts.

From my training and experience in business administration, I have adopted a personal and professional motto that suggests the most reasonable manner in which to accomplish any task. It is, "Use the most direct route, at the least cost, for the greatest amount of good." In a very practical sense, this is exactly what the Biblical Directionism Counseling model accomplishes.

It seems that God, as the Great Conserver, has provided us with a generic counseling model that takes the most direct and efficient route for bringing the greatest amount help and healing to individuals. This is not to suggest Biblical counseling is "easy." However, it does affirm that Biblical Directionism Counseling is the most reasonable, logical, and dependable method for bringing hope and healing to those who seek to find the **RATIONE ET VIA CERTUS**.

APPENDIX

A COMPARATIVE ANALYSIS OF BIBLICAL THEOLOGY AND HUMANISTIC PSYCHOLOGY

FOR A GREAT MANY CENTURIES, Biblical Theology was known as the "Queen of the sciences." However, by the end of the Nineteenth Century, theology had fallen from its long-held position of respect. Not long after the turn of the century, Chafer noted, "Theology, the greatest of all sciences, has fallen upon evil days. Between the rejection and ridicule of it by the so-called progressives and the neglect and abridgement of it by the orthodox, it, as a potent influence, is approaching the point of extinction." Chafer, Volume I., v.

Prior to its decline as an almost universally respected science, the study of theology provided man with the answers to the most fundamental and relevant questions of life. When man sought answers to the questions of creation, evil, and the possibility of life beyond body death, he turned to the Bible, theology's "Source Book."

During the past two hundred years, there has been an ever-increasing shift away from that almost universal acceptance of theology as the "Queen of the sciences." This shift is now so complete in today's world that theology is no longer universally regarded as a science at all. In fact, even at the graduate seminary level, theology is being crowded out of its rightful place in curriculum. This trend was already well established by the turn of the century. Not everyone at the seminary level recognized what was happening, but Dr. Lewis Sperry Chafer, founder and first president of Dallas Theological Seminary was forced to lament, "While the seminary student needs as much theology as ever, the trend, unfortunately, is to substitute philosophy, psychology, and sociology for theology." Ibid, viii.

During the years of theology's decline, another science was experiencing tremendous change and growth; psychology, in contrast with theology, was moving up to a place of great respect among the scientific disciplines.

Unlike theology, which has a simple and universally accepted definition of purpose - "the science of God and of relations between God and the universe" Bancroft, 13. - psychology is a difficult discipline to define. The following examples reveal something of the difficulty in coming to a generally held consensus.

> "Psychology is a disciplined attempt to explain, evaluate, and control behavior." Beacon Dictionary of Theology, 430.

> "The science that systematically studies and attempts to explain observable behavior and its relationship to the unseen mental processes that go on inside the organism and to external events in the environment." Kagan and Haverman, 595.

> "The Science which deals with human behavior, both normal and abnormal." Thorpe, 583.

> "Is it possible to provide a simple definition of such a diverse field? If such definition must rigorously include everything that is a part of psychology and exclude everything that is not, the answer is no. Probably the best

> definition is that psychology is the
> science of human and animal
> behavior." Hill, 2.

This apparent difficulty in defining exactly what psychology actually is presents a dilemma to those who would attempt any comparative analysis between psychology and theology. As Dr. William K. Kilpatrick has noted, "Psychology is a river with many branches and tributaries." Kilpatrick, 9.

Nevertheless, the field of psychology may be divided into at least two major elements. First, there is that element of psychology which relates to pure science or what may be considered as the biological/material functions. We may elaborate and suggest this first element of psychology "includes speech, minute muscle movements, glandular secretions - in short, every detectable or potentially detectable action or reaction of the individual." Hill, *Op. ct.*, 2-3.

The second element could be defined as that area of psychology which seeks to explain the whole of man, including his physical, mental, social, religious, and transcendental relationships to life.

Theology and psychology have no fundamental difficulties as they relate in the area of genuine science. It is when psychology begins to move out beyond its scientific parameters that it comes into direct conflict with theology. "Psychology as a science has a legitimate part to play in our society. It is another matter, however, when it wants to play every part and direct the drama as well." Kilpatrick, *Op. cit.*, 9.

That psychology has, in fact, moved far beyond its scientific parameters to become a competing philosophy with theology cannot really be doubted, even by reason of a cursory examination.

HUNT AND McMAHON HAVE CORRECTLY OBSERVED:

"Psychology, in contrast to Biblical counseling by very definition, can neither explain nor adequately deal with man as God created him, much less as the redeemed man is intended to be through Christ living in him. Science can deal with such things as nutritional deficiencies or chemical imbalances in the brain, but it has nothing to say about the mind, which is nonphysical.

Moreover, psychology not only pretends to bring 'science' to bear on problems which it cannot even define, much less solve, but it claims to meet needs that the Bible says it alone can provide. Thus, psychology is in the fullest sense a rival religion that can never be wedded to Christianity. Furthermore, Psychotherapy involves the danger that is implicit in all false religions." Hunt and McMahon, 191.

It is at the point where theology and psychology clash that we arrive at a definition which serves to make clear that theology and psychology are, in fact, opposing philosophies. However, let it be stated again that where psychology remains within the parameters of true science, there is no fundamental conflict with theology.

In order to delineate that element of psychology which is in diametric opposition to theology, the term "humanistic psychology" will be employed. For the purpose of this study, "humanistic psychology" refers to that element of psychology which crosses the borders of science and attempts to operate within the dominion of theology.

For further clarification, I will divide the definition into its two components.

1. Humanism (humanistic) - the doctrine that rejects supernaturalism and stresses the worth and determinism of man as supreme in the universe. The term comes from Latin "*humanitas*" (the human race). Beacon Dictionary of Theology, *Op. cit.*, 266-267

2. Psychology - the derivation of the word psychology, from the Greek words *'psyche'* and *'logia,'* suggests that psychology is the science of the mind. Hill, *Op. cit.*, 2.

Succinctly stated, humanistic psychology is that doctrine which holds the mind of man to be supreme and that no transcendental or metaphysical reality exists outside of the human mind.

A STUDY IN CONTRASTS

At the heart of biblical Theology, three great doctrines reveal the whole of what man's relationship to God and God's relationship to man are really all about. These three great doctrines deal with sin, salvation from sin, and life beyond the earthly grave.

While within the ranks of orthodox theologians there is room for certain differences of opinion, there can be no difference of opinion regarding sin, salvation, and life beyond the grave if that difference results in a denial of man's sinful nature, God's plan for man's salvation, and the reality of an eternal destiny for all mankind. For if such a denial existed, those denying would no longer qualify as being orthodox. Biblical orthodoxy declares the uncompromising truth of these three doctrines. It is not that other biblical doctrines are not as important, but if you deny any of these three, you have destroyed the reason for the Christian faith altogether.

Therefore, any philosophy which denies the biblical orthodoxy of sin, salvation, and life beyond the earthly grave denies, in effect, the Christian faith as a whole. Such denial ought to certainly qualify as a competing antithesis. Such a competing antithesis is warned of in Scripture.

> "See to it that no one takes you captive through hollow and deceptive philosophy, which depends on human tradition and the basic principles of this world rather than on Christ." Colossians 2:8

HAMARTIOLOGY AND HUMANISTIC PSYCHOLOGY

"That branch of theology which deals with the doctrine of sin is called 'hamartiology.' It claims a very large share of careful attention, since sin is man's basic problem... 'hamartia' is used as the basic generic term (Greek) for sin in the New Testament." Beacon Dictionary of Theology, *Op. cit.*, p. 483-484 The following brief statements are the salient of the Biblical doctrine of sin.

1. Nature proclaims it (Genesis 3:17).
2. Men acknowledge it (Psalm 51:5).
3. Law discovers it (Romans 3:20).
4. God declares it (Jeremiah 17:9).
5. Christ reveals it (I Timothy 1:15).
6. Experience proves it (Ecclesiastes 9:3).
7. No man can escape its inherited mark (Romans 3:23). Bancroft, *Op. cit.*, 214-217.

The Nature of sin in man is actually two-fold. First, there is the inherited element of sin often called "depravity." It is this depravity which makes man a sinner and causes him to sin. Depravity is universal with mankind. The second element of sin is that which is acted out, thought out, or by reason of neglect, left out. Again, this second element of sin is universal with mankind.

The basic premise of hamartiology is that man is inherently sinful and that, left totally to his own schemes and devices, will exhibit that sinfulness in all areas of life. As Jeremiah said, "The heart is deceitful above all things, and beyond cure. Who can understand it?" (17:9).

Not only is the mind of man inherently sinful, it is naturally disposed to rebellion against God. As St. Paul declared, "The sinful mind is hostile to God. It does not submit to God's law, nor can it do so." (Romans 8:7).

The theological answer to man's universal wickedness is that *he posesses a sinful nature*. The psychological answer to man's wickedness is altogether different; in fact, it is diametrically opposed to the Biblical doctrine of sin.

Louis P. Thorpe, in **THE PSYCHOLOGY OF MENTAL HEALTH**, suggested, "One of the major hazards of religious affiliations is that of being expected to live in harmony with certain conservative practices and taboos which, since they increase the likelihood of manifesting behavior which is regarded as being wrong, are likely to result in feelings of guilt (condemnation by the superego). Thorpe, *Op. Cit.*, 505.

Thorpe seems to be suggesting that religious restraints actually cause mental illness. He makes no reference to sin as a contributing cause, nor does he acknowledge it as the source of all wrong-doing. In fact, a careful search of his work fails to reveal even a hint that there may be something inherently wrong with mankind which is the principle cause of his misery. What is easy to find is his dislike for the church and its call to conservative moral restraints. Of the church he wrote:

> "It is evident, however, that religious intolerance and conflicts between sectarian dogmas, which in many instances lead people to regard as

> 'wrong' certain patterns of behavior
> which for the most part are acceptable in
> the larger society outside of the church,
> make for personality maladjustment and
> in some cases a serious degree of mental
> ill-health." *Ibid*, 505.

Thorpe, elsewhere in his work, quoted H. A. Overstreet's five-point suggestion as to why people fail to fit into the normal elements of society and properly mature. These are:

1. unrealistic self-estimates;
2. unrealistic estimates of others;
3. too much self-concern;
4. a false concept of authority;
5. a too-meager conception of the potentialities of life. *Ibid*, 258.

While even the most orthodox theologian might agree to some extent with these five barriers to normal development, where does sin fit into the picture? It is obvious that, from Thorpe's viewpoint, sin is a non-reality. Hunt and McMahon address this rejection of man's inherent sinfulness by noting:

> "The idea that man's innate goodness - of
> the innocent child that still resides within
> us all - is the cornerstone of psychology.
> Under that sponsorship, evangelical
> tradition is being replaced by a new
> humanistic view of man, which ridicules
> as 'worm theology' the former emphasis
> upon correction of sin, repentance, and
> humanity's unworthiness." Hunt and
> McMahon, *Op. cit.*, 192

Both Sigmund Freud and Carl Rogers denied the inherent sinfulness of man. "Freud's most fundamental premise was that man is not responsible for what he does; instead, someone else is. Rogers believed that man doesn't need divine revelation; he is autonomous. Rogers stressed human autonomy as essential to successful living." Adams, THE BIG UMBRELLA, 50-53.

This rejection of man's sinfulness is a foundational cornerstone of humanistic psychology. Thus, humanistic psychology has clearly become a competing religion alongside Christianity. There is absolutely no congruence between the Biblical doctrine of sin and humanistic psychology's dogma that man is essentially good.

Regarding this dichotomy, Merne A. Harris has noted:

> "This 'triad of morality' so described by David Belgum (Guilt, Where Psychology and Religion Meet, 17-34) is jeopardized by psychology's eagerness to replace God's immutable values with society's transient ones. Karl Menninger perceived this tendency in asking, 'Whatever became of sin?'" BEACON DICTIONARY OF THEOLOGY, *Op. cit.*, 430.

William Kirk Kilpatrick was associate professor of educational psychology at Boston College. His return to conservative Biblical values, along with his bold public stand for Christianity, had a type of lodestone effect upon other Christian mental health professionals. Dr. Kilpatrick comments on this dichotomy between sin and humanistic psychology's rejection thereof.

> "Christianity doesn't make much sense without sin. If we are not sinners, turned away from God, then there was no reason for God to become man, and no reason for Him to die. Our slavery to sin is the thing that Christ came to free us from. That is the most fundamental Christian belief. It follows that if you

have no consciousness of sin, you simply won't be able to see the point of Christianity. We can state the matter more strongly and say that once you grant the notion that people are sinless, you must admit that Christianity is all wrong."Kilpatrick, *Op. cit.*, 74.

Hamartiology and humanistic psychology are incompatible ideologies incapable of any sort of peaceful coexistence.

SOTERIOLOGY AND HUMANISTIC PSYCHOLOGY

Soteriology is the second of the three great doctrines of biblical theology. "Soteriology (soteria = salvation + logos + word) is that branch of Christian theology which treats the doctrines of salvation, including:

1. atonement for sin - the provision of salvation through Christ and;

2. salvation from sin - the application of salvation by the Spirit." Beacon Dictionary of Theology, *Op. cit.*, 494.

It reasons out that any concept of salvation requires a foundational belief in whatever it is from which one is to be saved. Since the foundational belief of soteriology is man's sinful condition, it follows that the likelihood of soteriology and humanistic psychology having anything in common is remote.

Generic to soteriology is the meritorious death of Christ on Calvary and His substitutionary position between man and God. Isaiah declared, "and the Lord has laid on Him the iniquity of us all" (Isaiah 53:6). In contrast to this, Louis P. Thorpe, former professor of educational psychology at the University of Southern

101

California, wrote:

> "Another aspect of the last-named problem (mental ill-health) is that of utilization of religion as a means of escape from reality, or as a dependency mechanism which encourages the individual to 'cast his burdens on the Lord' - and cease to do anything about them himself." Thorpe, *Op. Cit.*, 506-507.

However, "casting our burdens upon the Lord" is the whole point of why Christ came as the Saviour of mankind. Man is simply unable to save himself! Without a Saviour, man, in his sinful condition, would be forever consigned to eternal meaninglessness. This is precisely why Peter declared, "Cast all your anxiety on Him because He cares for you" (I Peter 5:7). This does not relieve man of his own personal responsibility. If Thorpe had been honest with his readers, he would have quoted the passage which immediately follows I Peter 5:7, that is, verses 8 and 9:

> *"Be self-controlled and alert. Your enemy the devil prowls around like a roaring lion looking for someone to devour. Resist him, standing firm in the faith. . ."*

At the heart of the doctrine of soteriology is the change of thinking that salvation brings into the life of the individual. Of this change Adams notes:

> "Change is possible; that conviction must be maintained as a foundational fact of Christian counseling. Radical change, the most radical change known to man, is described in the Scriptures as a 'new birth.' The use of this figure of speech indicates the radical nature of the change. Nothing less than an entirely new start

toward life is in view." Adams, THE
CHRISTIAN COUNSELOR'S MANUAL, 29.

In sharp contrast to Adams' statement regarding the
new birth, is Edward C. Tolman's concept of
"behavior-adjustments." Tolman believed that
adjustments to behavior (good or bad) were the result
of "the mental activity that occurs when an individual
is confronted by a problem. It is a kind of mental
running back and forth among various alternatives
and options as to how the problem might be dealt
with effectively." Hall and Nordby, 173.

While Tolman's concept is agreeable to matters dealing
with everyday decision-making, it fails to account for
the dramatic life-change that takes place as a result of
the new birth. Salvation is not a change of mind on the
part of man. Salvation is God in Christ, reordering man
so radically that the mind is directly reshaped as a
result of that change.

Both Freud and Jung espoused a humanistic doctrine of
inner healing which is diametric to the doctrine of
soteriology. "These two Freudian/Jungian ideas,
'psychic determinism' and the 'unconscious' form the
foundation of inner healing." Hunt and McMahon, Op.
cit., 184. Of course, if there is no real transcendent, no
metaphysical, then it reasons out that both the
conscious and subconscious mind of man are the
supreme instruments of healing and change. Stated yet
another way, we can say that if there is no
supernatural, there is no sin; if no sin, no need of a
Saviour, and if no need of a Saviour, no such thing as
salvation, only "psychic determinism."

It is clear, then, that soteriology and humanistic
psychology have no common ground upon which to
build a mutually beneficial structure. They are, in fact,
diametrically opposed.

ETERNITY AND HUMANISTIC PSYCHOLOGY

The great biblical doctrine of eternity is often confused with that element of theology called "eschatology." While the two are directly related, eschatology deals with the broader range of things that are yet to come. These would include such subjects as the Second Coming of Christ, the coming of the Antichrist, the millennium, and the events associated with it. For the purpose of this comparative analysis, eschatology is too broad a subject.

The great doctrine of eternity deals basically with the biblical teaching involving man's existence following bodily death. This teaching is divided into two equal parts. First, eternal life will be experienced by all who believe in Jesus Christ for the remission of sin and trust in Him as Saviour and Lord. Second, everlasting life will be experienced by all who refuse to believe in Jesus Christ for the remission of sin and who also refuse to trust in Him as Saviour and Lord. That is, believer and nonbeliever (all human beings of all space/time relationships) will live forever in an eternal destiny of their own choosing. Those who have trusted in Christ will experience eternity in the immediate presence of God (heaven). Those who reject Christ will experience eternity forever banished from the presence of God (hell).

The great Biblical doctrine of eternity affirms man as an everlasting, never-dying entity of personal, conscious life. It further affirms that the present existence is the space/time period during which man must come to a willing personal decision to accept Jesus Christ as Lord and Saviour or to reject Him as such. This is why, for Christianity, all life has special meaning, purpose, and importance. It is also why the moral and ethical absolutes of the Bible must be regarded as non-negotiable and universally required. For the Christian, there are certain parameters, borders, limits, restraints, and, yes, rules and regulations. In short, immutable requisites which cannot be ignored without suffering eternal loss.

That this concept of eternity is unacceptable to humanistic psychology is well-stated by one of its proponents.

> "Conflicts relating to religion seen in certain forms of mental illness include concern over so-called 'unpardonable sin,' the 'sins of the flesh as against those of the spirit,' over scrupulous adherence to orthodox dogmas, confusion of deity with self, and preoccupation with an allegedly impending event such as the end of the world, or the Second Coming of Christ.

> Religious groups which isolate their members in an 'in-group' and severely criticize other's beliefs, those which demand severe disciplines not characteristic of the general social culture, and those which overemphasize the threat of 'sin' and rewards of the supposed 'life hereafter' as a substitute for enjoyment of life in the present are likely to foster mental ill-health." Thorpe, *Op. cit.*, 506.

Sigmund Freud, although criticized severely by some, is still the undisputed guiding light of the science of psychology. Lionel Trilling said of Freud, "Freud as a person stands before us with an exceptional distinctness and significance, and it is possible to say of him that there is no great figure of modern times who, seen as a developing mind and temperament, is of such singular interest." Jones, Introduction, 1. And yet, Freud had absolutely no faith in any sort of literal eternal existence for man. In fact, his biographer,

Ernest Jones, said of Freud, "There is no reason to think that Freud ever cudgeled his brains about the purpose of the universe - he was always an unrepentant atheist." *Ibid*, 23.

Carl Jung, along with Sigmund Freud, is considered by many in the field of psychology, to be one of the two great minds of our time. Jung, a Swiss psychiatrist, was the son of a Lutheran Reformed clergyman. While Jung's entire life's work was deeply involved in the supernatural (a point at which he and Freud experienced sharp disagreement) and though Jung was considered a deeply religious person, it must be understood that for Jung religion was just that - religion. "Jung did not confine himself to direct practice but let his mind range widely in order to experience the testimony of spiritual-religious experience, the traditional wisdom and practices of Asia, as well as Christian-Gnosticism and the alchemy of the Middle Ages." Weher, 8.

Because Jung had no true theological base, he regarded all religions in nearly the same light. But what of his belief in the eternal destiny of man? Whatever his belief really was (which is nearly impossible to pin down to anything specific), one thing is certain - his open rejection of Jesus Christ as God's Son and Saviour of the world is undeniable. Jung, himself, said, "All that about Lord Jesus was always suspect to me, and I never really believed it." Ibid, p. 73. But the Apostle Paul said of Jesus, "He appeared in a body, was vindicated by the Spirit, was seen by angels, was preached to the nations, was believed on in this world, was taken up to glory" (I Timothy 3:16).

It is an easy thing to find deep religious roots among psychology's major framers. Ivan Pavlov and Carl Rogers were both one-time seminary students. Edward Thorndike, Carl Jung, and Gardner Murphy were sons of Christian clergymen. Hall and Nordby, *Op. cit.* Yet, none of these men advocated the Biblical doctrine of eternal life through Jesus Christ.

Why, then, is there so much tension between the Biblical doctrine of eternity and the psychological establishment's world-view of man? The answer is simply that humanistic psychology denies the very thing for which Christ died.

> *"We believe that Jesus died and rose again and so we believe that God will bring with Jesus those who have fallen asleep in Him."* I Thessalonians 4:14.

SUMMARY

When the three great doctrines of Biblical Theology are compared with humanistic psychology, it becomes unavoidably clear that they are opposing forces. They are, in fact, diametrically opposed in every way. What reason, then, could a biblical counselor possibly give for adapting the principles and practices of humanistic psychology or lauding its major framers? Or, as by the Apostle Paul stated:

> *"Do not be yoked together with unbelievers. For what do righteousness and wickedness have in common? Or what fellowship can light have with darkness? What harmony is there between Christ and Belial? What does a believer have in common with an unbeliever?"* II Corinthians 6:14-15.

The Evolutionary Influence

By the term "evolutionary influence," I mean to suggest that the science of psychology has been heavily influenced by the theory that man (as in the case of all other life forms) is merely the biological product of the modifications taking place in the successive generations of the human animal. Further, that man is not the completed product of special creation whereby God brought him into existence as biologically mature and complete. The theory of evolution views man as the present apex of the biological progression of the animal order.

The Darwinian Foundation

British naturalist, Charles Darwin (1809-1882), is the father of modern evolutionary concepts, even though the theory of evolution was not original with Darwin. "Evolutionary philosophy had been increasingly influential in the so-called Christian world for many decades before Charles Darwin, but his famous book 'The Origin of the Species by Natural Selection' became the great watershed. Before 1859, creationism and the biblical world view still dominated Western thought. Within one decade after its publication, however, Darwinism was widely accepted...and the world has never been the same since." Morris, 103.

Before the full influence of Darwinism, man was largely viewed as the apex of God's creative purposes and, as such, was the special object of His love. What Darwinism did was to substitute this theological concept with a so-called scientific one that provided naturalistic explanations in the place of the supernatural.

An interesting fact about Charles Darwin (one not widely published by his proponents) is that he possessed no academic credentials whatever to qualify him as a natural scientist or biologist. In fact, Darwin's only academic degree was a degree in theology from Christ College. Switching from an early and limited study of the field of medicine, Darwin enrolled as a divinity student in the hopes of preparing for the Christian ministry where he came under the influence of evolutionary philosophy and eventually surrendered his faith. Ibid, 11, 402. Yet, it was upon this unproved and unscientific hypothesis, improvised by an apostate theology student, that an entire scientific discipline has built its monolith.

HUXLEIAN DEVELOPMENT

Thomas H. Huxley (1825-1895), was a colleague and protagonist of Charles Darwin. As a widely respected scientist (though lacking a formal education) , Huxley gave to Darwin's works the credibility they would have otherwise eventually lacked. Huxley was also better prepared to disseminate their evolutionary philosophy. As the theory of evolution took on increasing sophistication, it moved rapidly away from any association with the Bible.

In 1869, Huxley coined the term "agnosticism." "He used this term with reference to the existence of the religious object, or God. He took neither an affirmative nor a negative position, but simply said that our judgment must be held in suspension on this question. We do not have sufficient evidence to conclude whether God exists or not, according to Huxley and other agnostics." Young, 61.

FREUDIAN APPLICATION

Austrian psychoanalyst, Sigmund Freud (1856-1939), was powerfully influenced by both Darwin and Huxley. Huxley's "Introduction to Science" was a favorite of Freud's, and a singular honor of his later life was being invited, in 1931, by the University of London to deliver the annual Huxley Lecture. Though not actually able to accept the invitation, Freud considered it a great honor. Jones, *Op. cit.*, 113, 471.

The influence of Charles Darwin upon Freud was likewise profound. Freud once wrote, "The theories of Darwin, which were then of topical interest, strongly attracted me, for they held out hopes of an extraordinary advance in our understanding of the world." Ibid, 22. Freud eventually came to believe man was totally a biological creature. He saw man through a Darwinian/Huxleian mind-set. "Freud's view of man's development is in part an evolutionary one. Man's biological urges are part of his evolved nature." Schell, 38.

As arguably the major framer of what is today the humanistic school of psychology, it is critically important to note of Sigmund Freud that he was both an evolutionist and an atheist. It is also critically important to note the two men who influenced him most from the natural sciences were also men devoid of real spiritual roots. Darwin was an apostate to Christianity; Huxley was an agnostic.

THE FAILURE OF THE EVOLUTIONARY INFLUENCE

To many in the field of psychology, the evolutionary influence has provided a new and enlightened path upon which man has entered into better and brighter days. But, is it an enlightened path leading us to brighter and better days, or is it simply a primrose path leading ultimately to an already opened Pandora's box?

To answer this question, it is necessary to look back to what the evolutionary mentality has had to say about yesterday. In partial answer to this question, Rushdoony had noted, "For the Darwinist, history is the product of impersonal biological forces . . . for the Freudian, psychological and unconscious." Rushdoony, 14. What this evolutionary influence means in practical terms is that history is de-personalized, and man is de-personalized along with it." *Ibid*, 14.

If the evolutionary influence cannot tell us where we have been and why, how can it possibly tell us where we are to go and how? It cannot! The fact is, the evolutionary influence and its marriage to humanistic psychology has been a disastrous and colossal failure.

Dr. William Kirk Kilpatrick has observed:

"Despite the creation of a virtual army of psychiatrists, psychologists, psychometrists, counselors, and social workers, there has been no let up in the ratio of mental illness, suicide, alcoholism, drug addiction, child abuse, divorce, murder, and general mayhem. Contrary to what one might expect in a society so carefully analyzed and attended to by mental health experts, there has been an increase in all these categories." Kilpatrick, *Op. cit.*, p. 31

The fault lies not in the mental health professions themselves; they are filled with well-meaning, compassionate, and caring people. Rather, the fault lies in the destructive evolutionary influence within their accepted systems. It is an influence which has attempted to dethrone God and discard His Word. This is doomed to failure. His Word is and always will be the "**RATIONE ET VIA CERTUS.**"

> *"There is a way that seems right to a man,*
> *but in the end it leads to death."*
> Proverbs 14:12

*"Heaven and earth will pass away, but
My words will never pass away."*
Luke 21:33

Hunt, David and McMahon, T. A., 1986, The Seduction Of Christianity. (Eugene, Oregon: Harvest House Publishers).

Hyder, O. Quentin, 1976, The Christian's Handbook Of Psychiatry. (NY: Fleming H. Revell Company).

Jones, Ernest, 1963, The Life And Work Of Sigmund Freud. (Garden City, NY: Anchor Books Doubleday and Company, Inc.).

Kagan, Jerome and Havemann, Ernest, 1972, Psychology: An Introduction. (NY: Harcourt Brace Jovanovich, Inc.).

Kilpatrick, William Kirk, 1983, Psychological Seduction. (NY: Thomas Nelson Publishers).

Knapp, Martin Wells, 1892, Impressions. (Cincinnati, OH: God's Revivalist Office, Revivalis Publishing House).

Latourette, Kenneth Scott, 1965, Christianity Through The Ages. (NY: Harper and Row Publishers).

Menninger, Karl, 1961, Theory Of Psychoanalytic Technique. (NY: Science Editions, Inc.).

Morris, Henry M., 1985, The Biblical Basis For Modern Science. (Grand Rapids, Michigan: Baker Book House).

Narramore, Clyde M., 1975, The Psychology Of Counseling. (Grand Rapids, MI: Zondervan Publishing House).

Purkiser, W.T., 1955, Exploring The Old Testament. (Kansas City, MO: Beacon Hill Press of Kansas City).

Purkiser, W.T., 1960, Exploring Our Christian Faith. (Kansas City,MO: Beacon Hill Press of Kansas city).

Purkiser, W.T., 1969, The New Testament Image Of The Ministry. (Grand Rapids, MI: Baker book House).

Ramm, Bernard L. and Others, 1976, Hermeneutics. (Grand Rapids, MI: Baker Book House).

Rushdoony, Rousas, 1979, The Biblical Philosophy Of History. (Phillipsburg, New Jersey: Presbyterian and Reformed Publishing Company).

Salter, Andrew, 1975, The Case Against Psycho' Analysis. (NY: Henry Holt and Company).

Schell, Robert E., Chief Coordinator, 1975, Developmental Psychology Today. (NY: Random House).

Seamands, David A., 1983, Putting Away Childish Things. (Weaton, IL: Victor Brooks).

Smith, Timothy L., 1957, Revivalism And Social Reform. (Baltimore, MD: The John's Hopkins University Press).

Strong, James, 1967, The Exhaustive Concordance Of The Bible. (Chicago, IL: Moody Press).

Taylor, Richard S., Editor, 1983, Beacon Dictionary Of Theology. (Kansas City, Mo.: Beacon Hill Press of Kansas City).

1976, The Analytical Greek Lexicon. (Grand Rapids, MI: Zondervan Publishing House).

1979, The NIV Interlinear Hebrew-English Old Testament. Vol I, Genesis-Deuteronomy. (Grand Rapids, MI: Zondervan Publishing House).

1978, The Holy Bible, The New International Version. (Grand Rapids, MI: New York International Bible Society).

1975, The Zondervan Parallel New Testament In Greek And English. (Grand Rapids, MI: Zondervan Bible Publishers).

1980, Theological Wordbook Of The Old Testament. Vols I,II. (Chicago, IL: Moody Press).

Thorpe, Louis P., 1960, The Psychology Of Mental Health. (NY: The Ronald Press Company).

Torrey, R.A., 1972, The Power Of Prayer. (Grand Rapids, MI: Zondervan Publishing House).

Uhrig, Paul E., 1980, How To Live Your Own Life. (Richmond, VA: Paul E. Uhrig).

Vincent, Marvin R., 1977, Word Studies In The New Testament. Vols I-IV. (Grand Rapids, MI: Wm.B. Eerdmans Publishing Company).

Vine, W.W., Vine's Expository Dictionary Of New Testament Words. (McLean,VA: MacDonald Publishing Company).

Weber, Gerhard, (Translated by W. H. Hargraves), 1971, Portrait Of Jung. (NY: Herder and Herder).

Wicks, Robert J., Helping Others. (Randnor, PA: Chilton Book Company).

Williams, R.T., 1939, Pastor And People. (Kansas City, MO: Nazarene Publishing House).

Williams, R.T., Relationships In Life. (Kansas City, MO: Nazarene Publishing House).

Williamson, G.B., Overseers Of The Flock. (Kansas City, MO: Beacon Hill Press of Kansas City).

Young, Warren C., 1982, A Christian Approach To Philosophy. (Grand Rapids, MI: Baker Book House).

For further information Contact: The Master's Library Press, P.O. Box 5009, Evansville, IN 47716-5009. Or call 1-812-471-0611.

Printed in the United States
1420900006B/1-117

BIBLIOGRAPHY

Adams, Jay E., 1972, The Big Umbrella. (Nutley, NJ: Presbyterian and Reformed Publishing House).

Adams, Jay E., 1970, Competent To Counsel. (Phillipsburg, NJ: Presbyterian and Reformed Publishing Company).

Adams, Jay E., 1970, The Christian Counselor's Manual. (Phillipsburg, NJ: Presbyterian and Reformed Publishing House).

Bacus, William, 1985, Telling The Truth To Troubled People. Minneapolis, MN: Bethany House Publishers).

Bancroft, Emery H., 1976, Christian Theology. (Grand Rapids, MI: Zondervan Publishing House).

Barnette, Henlee H., 1961, Introducing Christian Ethics. (Nashville, TN: Broadman Press).

Berkhof, L., 1975, Principles Of Biblical Interpretation. (Grand Rapids, MI: Baker Book House).

Berlin, Irving N., 1979, Depression In Children And Adolescents. Alfred P. French. (NY: Human Science Press).

Bounds, E.M., Purpose In Prayer. (Chicago, IL: Moody Press).

Brandt, Henry R., 1969, The Struggle For Peace. (Wheaton, IL: Scripture Press Publications).

Chafer, Lewis Sperry. 1983, Chafer's Systematic Theology, Eight Volumes. (Dallas, TX: Dallas Seminary Press).

Chapman, J.B., The Touch Of Jesus. (Kansas City, MO: Beacon Hill Press).

Clarke, Adam, 1976, Commentary On The Bible. Ed. and Abridged, Ralph Earle (Grand Rapids, MI: Baker Book House).

Cramer, George H., 1967, First And Second Peter. (Chicago, IL: Moody Press).

Geisler, Norman L., 1982, Philosophy Of Religion. (Grand Rapids, MI: Zondervan Publishing House).

Grensted, L.W., 1952, The Psychology Of Religion. (NY: Oxford University Press).

Gundry, Robert G., 1981, A Survey Of The New Testament. (Grand Rapids, MI: Zondervan Publishing House).

Hall, Calvin S. and Nordby, Vernon J.,1974, A Guide To Psychologists And Their Concepts. (San Francisco, CA: W.H. Freeman and Company).

Henry,Matthew, 1976, Commentary On The Whole Bible. Ed. Leslie F. Church. (Grand Rapids, MI: Zondervan Publishing House).

Hill, Winfred, 1970, Psychology: Principles And Problems. (NY: J.B. Lippincott Company).

ABOUT THE AUTHOR

Dennis D. Frey, A.B.S., Nazarene Bible College; M.Min., M.Div., D.Min., Th.D., Trinity Theological Seminary; M.B.A., D.B.A., California Coast University.

Initially trained in business, Dr. Frey began serving in Christian ministry in 1972. A former pastor and founder of a biblical counseling center, he has been teaching at the college level since 1985. Dr. Frey is currently serving as President of Master's Divinity School and Master's Graduate School of Divinity, Evansville, Indiana, **www.mdivs.edu.**